SOAR INTO JOY

A Combat Pilot's Wisdom on Falling in Love with Your Life

LOREE "ROWDY" DRAUDE

Published by
Hybrid Global Publishing
333 E 14th Street
#3C
New York, NY 10003

Manufactured in the United States of America, or in the United Kingdom when distributed elsewhere.

Draude, Loree.
SOAR into Joy
      ISBN: 978-1-957013-95-4
      eBook: 978-1-957013-96-1
      LCCN: 2023912233

Cover design by: Julia Kuris
Copyediting by: Wendie Pecharsky
Interior design by: Suba Murugan
Author photo by: Jeremy Folmer
Logo design by: Chris Wojcicki
Back cover Author photo by: Jon Anderson

www.loreedraude.com

"A former combat pilot, Silicon Valley manager, and start-up executive – and now leadership coach and developer for tech players – Loree Draude graphically comes to grip with her own fears and setbacks. Through absorbing accounts of her failures but also her comebacks, she helps us transcend our own troubles to find joy in all we experience. Here's your playbook for soaring through life."

– Michael Useem, Faculty Director of the McNulty
Leadership Program, Wharton School,
University of Pennsylvania, and
author of *The Edge:
How 10 CEOs Learned to Lead*

"From her decades spent as a U.S. Navy combat pilot and then as a leadership coach to hundreds in Silicon Valley, Loree leverages her pioneering experiences and unique vantage point to share her courageous wisdom, intelligent humor and pragmatic advice for how to create a life that is joy-filled, both professionally and personally. A must-read for anyone open to crafting a more authentic existence while achieving your maximum potential."

— Jenna C. Fisher, Russell Reynolds Associates partner
and Wall Street Journal best-selling author of
"To the Top: How Women in Corporate
Leadership Are Rewriting the
Rules for Success"

"In "Soar Into Joy," Loree fearlessly shares her journey with candid vulnerability and insightful wisdom, providing a flight plan to overcome fears, find fulfillment, and soar to new heights. Through personal stories and practical guidance, she invites readers to discover their own path to living a life of purpose and joy."

— Eric Karpinski, author of "Put Happiness
to Work: 7 Strategies to Elevate Engagement
for Optimal Performance"

"Loree shares real, raw and relevant life filled wisdom stories in such a compelling manner, that I found myself reflecting deeper on the life I long to be living...and is that not the job of a great inspirational book. Read it and soar more! Promise!"

— Dr. Rick Tamlyn, MCC, CPCC—
Hay House author of Play Your Bigger Game.

"Beautifully written. Witty, fun, powerful, instructive. Rowdy Draude uses her experiences as one of the first women to fly in a navy combat squadron to teach us how we can embrace fear and failure in order to S.O.A.R through life. A must read for anyone about to embark on a new challenge—personal or professional—who wants to map out a flight plan for success!"

— Cari Costanzo, Social and Cultural Anthropologist,
Stanford University

Dedication

This book is dedicated to my children, my parents, my brothers, my fellow veterans, and my friends, who have all supported me to SOAR.

CONTENTS

"I'd rather regret the things I've done than the things I haven't done."

— LUCILLE BALL

INTRODUCTION

When people look at me, who do they see? People who know me tell me they see a strong, independent woman, who used to land jets on an aircraft carrier, and then went on to a flourishing career, leading teams in Silicon Valley technology companies, and because of her prior successes, is now pursuing her dream of living a creative life as an artist, writer, and coach. My followers on social media and my executive coaching clients see a successful woman leader who has expertly navigated the world of male-dominated workplaces of my own volition, working tirelessly to achieve success by leveraging my above-average intellect, indefatigable inner drive, and unwavering perseverance.

Well, that's a bunch of baloney.

Okay, it's partially baloney. Yes, I worked hard, studied, and paid attention, but my success wasn't a linear "up and to the right" graph over time; there were plenty of peaks and dips along the way.

This book is about what has helped me overcome the fears I have (and that I believe we all have) in order to live a life I love, despite the challenges I've experienced. I wrote this book to pass on what has worked for me in hopes it will help someone else who is struggling. Many books inspired and guided me (see the

Resources chapter at the end), and I hope what you're about to read will likewise have a positive influence on your life.

Fear pervades our lives, magnified by the news media and assumptions we've grown up believing. We need to know that we can make a difference. Please don't make me trot out the story about the child on the beach throwing starfish back into the ocean[1]. My point is that we each can make a positive difference that has a bigger impact than we realize because we *are* all connected.

Think about it: The chair you're sitting on while you read this (unless you're listening to the audio version) was made by someone else. The roads we drive on were constructed by people, likely years ago, maybe even decades. Our food was farmed, gathered, packaged, shipped, and stocked by fellow human beings. Unless you're living in a cabin in the woods, growing your own food, and weaving your own clothes, you are not living in this world alone, no matter how independent you think you are. We all need one another.

I've experienced much fear, as you might imagine, but not the type you might expect. Yes, it was terrifying to land a multimillion-dollar jet on a pitching flight deck at night with no visible horizon and crappy weather, especially since I was responsible for not just me but the three other people in my crew who counted on me to get them home safely. And I knew that if I screwed up the landing, I might endanger the sailors working on

---

1 Really? Okay, it goes like this: Someone is walking along a beach covered with starfish that have washed up on the shore. This person feels sad seeing all these poor starfish that will most certainly dry out in the sunlight and die. "Oh well, there's no way to save all these starfish," the person thinks, but then they see a child picking up a starfish and chucking it back into the ocean. The child is doing this one by one. The person says, "Are you nuts? There are hundreds of dying starfish here. You can't possibly make a difference." And the child responds: "I just made a huge difference to that one starfish." BOOM.

the flight deck. And because I was one of the first women to fly in a combat jet squadron, I knew that if I screwed up, I'd make it more difficult for any woman following in my footsteps.

But that's not the fear I'm talking about. I'm talking about my fear of not being or having enough. I mean the fear of not being financially successful enough to afford a home and food, of not being attractive enough to find a mate, not being smart enough to be hired for jobs I want, not being strong enough to weather life's challenges, not being vigilant enough to not be taken advantage of… I could go on and on about not. being. enough.

It's the fear of failure. We get these messages every day from the news media and advertising: "Buy this product or service because you need to be healthier, thinner, better-looking, more prepared, better-armed" or "Here are all the terrible things happening in the world, and we're letting you know so you can be 'informed' and prepared, and you'll likely tune in, which will give us more advertising dollars if more 'eyeballs' are on us, which we need because we need more money because we're afraid that we ourselves won't have enough." I know they never actually say that, but isn't that what it's about?

This book was born from failure.

A few years ago, when one of my children was struggling with school and life in general, I wrote a letter to them with a list of the major failures of my life. I wanted them to understand and appreciate that I didn't just roll out of bed and land an awesome job at a company like Google. There was a long path to get there that was full of "failures" and "mistakes."

Here's my list (as of 2023; I'm sure I'll be adding more!):

- I tried out for Little League and didn't make the major league team (12-year-olds), so I had to play the entire season on the minor league team with eight-year-old boys. This was socially mortifying for a pre-teen girl.

- I ran for junior class president and lost.
- I copied my friend's homework in 12th grade because I didn't have time to do it myself and got busted for it.
- I failed the obstacle course in flight school because I couldn't run through the sand fast enough. I had to practice every day for several weeks. It was painful, I absolutely hate running, but I had to pass the obstacle course in order to become an aviator.
- I drove home while intoxicated as a junior in high school and was grounded for a month. Thank God that was all that happened.
- I was dumped by my boyfriend in high school for my best friend.
- I failed a training flight in flight school.
- I scored in the bottom 10 percent for landing grades in my air wing when I joined my fleet squadron on the aircraft carrier. (Eighteen months later, I was in the top 10 percent and earned a patch for it.)
- I barely passed four of my 22 classes in business school.
- I completely bombed my interview in business school to work at Goldman Sachs. More on that later.
- I got divorced.
- I was fired from a job.
- I was laid off.
- I screwed up important relationships because of my own insecurities.
- I had to shut down a company I founded because we couldn't create a minimally viable product in time to raise more money.
- I didn't get the promotion I was expecting.

How did I overcome these setbacks?

How did I persevere when life wasn't going the way I wanted?

I found myself in the seemingly bottomless pit of fear about 11 years ago. I was in the middle of a divorce, and the startup where I worked laid me off. I worried about my ability to feed my kids and afford a home in ridiculously expensive Silicon Valley. With the help of an amazing coach (thank you, Katie Wurtz) and a therapist (thank you, Elizabeth Dumanian), I challenged my assumptions and recognized a few facts:

1. Even though I was "on my own" as a single mom, it didn't mean I was alone; in fact, I was fortunate to have an incredibly supportive family and a great network of friends who were there for me during that difficult time.
2. I was incredibly fortunate and privileged to have a solid education, rich work experience, and a supportive business network to tap into.
3. My world had been rocked, and I needed to update my perspective on life through some deep personal work, including therapy and a buttload of self-help books. BTW, I love lists. You're going to see many lists in this book. #virgo

This book is about what raised me out of my fear-based life, created energy to move forward, and soar into a life of fulfillment.

Note that I did not say "happiness" or "joy," even though that word is in the book title. "Joy" is an aspirational goal—something unattainable permanently in life but something we can aspire to experience as much as possible.

Some of the technology companies I worked for had vision statements; for example, Google's is "to provide access to the world's information in one click." This guides decisions on the products they make and their strategy, with the understanding that they'll likely never be able to provide access to ALL the world's information in ONLY one click, but they aspire to that.

Similarly, I aspire to live a joyful life, knowing that my life will have challenges and disappointments along the way and that I will never be 100 percent happy.

While I am incredibly happy most of the time, I don't consider happiness the goal. I could live on a beach, eat moon pies, and be extremely happy, but I'd be bored. I want to squeeze every last drop I can out of this life, and if that's the kind of life you want to live, then keep reading. This book is about how I learned to dance with fear, relax its firm grip on my mind, and started to SOAR.

Why am I writing this? I asked myself this very question many times while writing it. Who am I to think I have anything to add to the many self-help and leadership books that are already gathering dust on bookshelves worldwide?

The answer is: There's only one me, and if anything I share in this book about my experience helps one fellow human being to feel more hopeful, appreciated, inspired, or happy, then the effort of writing this has been worth it.

I found inspiration in others' books during the difficult periods of my life, and I hope that, in turn, I can inspire others.

As a student naval aviator, I learned about flying jets from different instructors, who each shared their unique tips and tricks they'd honed from years of flying.

I benefitted from their wisdom, understanding that no single instructor knows everything about how to best pilot an aircraft. Similarly, I view myself as a guide, not a guru. I hope my book is one tool in your life toolkit to complement other resources that you find helpful and inspiring.

I initially thought about writing a book to share lessons on leadership I've learned over the years, as I've been fortunate to lead many teams in my military and technology careers. I've utilized that experience to coach hundreds of executives, founders, and managers, so I thought it would be helpful to impart that knowledge to anyone who might pick up this book and benefit from it.

However, my executive coaching clients have found the personal "life" coaching to be the most transformative. Every leader is a human being with their own struggles, strengths, blind spots, and imperfections. Leadership is a skill that we exhibit when we are supporting and influencing a team, and that skill can be better optimized by a person working on their own development. To return to the "soaring" metaphor, an aircraft that has the latest technology and receives regularly scheduled maintenance and refueling will go much farther than a neglected airplane. Similarly, I felt that sharing the concepts that have helped me with my personal development and that I share with my clients would help build a solid foundation for leaders and anyone who wants to find more fulfillment in their life.

I haven't had an obvious or easy journey. Along the way, I've battled depression, had my heart broken, been fired from jobs, had weeks where I barely ate because I was struggling financially, suffered through my children being bullied on social media, and was stabbed in the back at work. What helped me get through it was coaching, therapy, advice, friends, and family I could lean on.

By sharing stories from my life, I hope to help you get unstuck, so you dare to do something you've always wanted to try but were afraid to. I wrote this book to pass on the inspiration I found while pursuing a life that fulfills me and to give you tools to achieve your dreams and live your life with as much joy as possible.

How to Use This Book

I've identified four themes that have enabled me to soar in life. Conveniently, they form an acronym of…wait for it…

S-O-A-R.

Shocking, I know, right?

There are many self-help and management books are on the market, so why is this book right for you?

Honestly, I don't know if it will be right for you. Yeah, I've never been all that great at selling.

If you're like me, it can be frustrating to hear so much advice, often conflicting, from self-proclaimed experts in a field. In one ear, you hear, "Be authentic!" while in the other, you hear, "Fake it 'til you make it!", "Lean in!" but "Don't get too attached to outcomes." "Be commanding!" but "Be empathetic!" Yikes! Who to believe? What to do?

I say, "Go with what feels right for *you*." Maybe some of the themes in this book will resonate with you, or maybe, when you read them, you'll think, "Hell, no, that's crazy talk, and I'd never do that," to which I say, "Awesome! You're becoming more self-aware, which is the "S" in SOAR. So… hah! You *should* read this book! Maybe I'm not so bad at sales after all.

What I do know is that I have unique stories to share that I hope will inspire you, just as I've found inspiration from hearing unique stories of people who have struggled and succeeded. I enjoy learning by listening to others' experiences and extracting the lessons I think could help me.

Are You Ready to SOAR?

When you SOAR, you are in that space where you're present in the moment, honoring your values and feeling fulfilled. It's like the concept of Flow that Mihaly Csikszentmihalyi describes in his bestselling book, *Flow: The Psychology of Optimal Experience*.[2] I've found four main components that enable me to find that space where I SOAR:

* **S**elf-Awareness
* **O**penness
* **A**ppreciation
* **R**esponsibility

Each of the following chapters represents one of my SOARing ideals. I'll share some stories from my military experience and my years working in the tech industry and at startups so you can see how it can influence you. I'll also share tactical information about how I solved business and personnel issues with companies. I hope you can take these ideas and work them into your toolset to improve your life.

At the end of each chapter, you'll find "Your Flight Plan." Every day in the Navy, we planned our day according to the Air Plan. This daily document listed the flights, who was flying together, the missions, and any important meetings we had to attend. Your Flight Plan is a summary of the takeaways from each chapter, along with some suggested exercises to help you put these concepts into practice.

"We are like islands in the sea, separate on the surface but connected in the deep."

—WILLIAM JAMES

---

2 Mihaly Csikszentmihalyi, *Flow: The Psychology of Optimal Experience* (New York: Harper & Row, 1990).

Chapter 1

WHAT DOES IT MEAN TO SOAR?

"One can never consent to creep when one feels an impulse to soar."

—HELEN KELLER

When you hear the word *soar*, what comes to mind? I envision birds, their wings outspread, seemingly floating in the air as they scan the ground for their next meal. Sometimes, they hover aloft for what feels like an impossible time, never having to flap their wings to generate lift.

I love seeing birds soaring because it reminds me that I, too, can design my life in a way that optimizes the lift underneath my wings and stays in a place of resonance. *Merriam-Webster* defines *soar* as "to ascend to a higher or more exalted level." My definition is "to fly with joy."

Let me start with a story of one of my most challenging night flights onboard an aircraft carrier. It's one of my favorite stories to share in a keynote speech because it illustrates perseverance and the power of finding joy.

We were getting ready to take off on a mission hundreds of miles away from land. The weather was not great. There was no visible horizon, as the moon was hidden behind a thick layer of clouds.

As we were taxiing toward the catapult for takeoff, one of the generators on our jet stopped working. I say "our" because I flew with a crew: a COTAC (a naval flight officer – NFO – who sits to the right of the pilot. NFOs do not control the movement of the aircraft), a TACCO (an NFO who sits in the back of the jet and manages the weapons and sonobuoys) and an aircrewman (an enlisted sailor who works with the TACCO to listen to submarines with the aforementioned sonobouys). The jet I was flying, the S-3B Viking, had two engines, each powering a separate generator, so we had backup power. We were able to restart it, but it shut off again. We weren't sure what was happening, but we could fly as long as we had one generator.

We decided to keep going. I kept cycling the generator switch, hoping it would keep working. We got up to the catapult to get ready to take off. Both generators were working fine, and things were looking up. Once we did our final cockpit checks, with the engines at full power, I turned our exterior lights on, indicating to the catapult officer that we were ready to fly. The catapult officer released the pistons that held us in place, and our jet was slung down the flight deck and thrown into the air.

As we left the carrier, we felt a thud, and instantaneously, *all of the lights in the cockpit went out.* We were in complete darkness. Shit!

Only two malfunctions can cause the electricity in the cockpit to fail. One is a dual engine failure; the other is a dual generator failure.

If you lose both engines on a catapult shot, you have two seconds before the jet hits the water below, so you must eject immediately.

But if you lose both generators, you have engines. You still have power so that you can fly. But you may not have electricity or lights.

As soon as all the lights went out, I felt I still had working engines. There wasn't the "wind down," the slowing drone sound of engines that had quit, and the nose of the aircraft didn't start to drop.

I immediately yelled to the COTAC, "I have control!" so he wouldn't pull the ejection handle. I had to yell because no electricity equals no intercom or radio either.

I yelled, "APU!" which let him know he needed to get our auxiliary power unit (APU) working as soon as possible, so we could have lights and be able to see. Because he was an experienced NFO, his hand was already pulling the APU handle as I shouted the next step in the checklist. I focused on keeping us out of the water, and he focused on getting us some electricity.

I always carried a flashlight in my torso harness and turned it on the red night setting before takeoff in case of an emergency like this — a tip I'd learned from an instructor pilot. I turned it toward the instrument panel and saw the analog engine gauges working.

We were going to be fine.

Most importantly, I could see the jet's nose-high attitude. We were rapidly climbing away from the water. The COTAC got the APU started. The APU dropped down from the belly of the jet so the airflow could turn its blades and generate electricity. The lights in the cockpit returned.

As the lights came on, I saw the jet was at a high as possible angle of attack to get us away from the water without stalling. We were able to get one of the generators started, but the other wouldn't come back online. I called back to the squadron to update them on our status, expecting to be called back for a landing. But instead, I was told to carry on our mission, and they'd see us in an hour and a half.

Welcome to the fleet! This isn't the Training Command anymore. You have to fly your mission, even when conditions aren't ideal.

We had the minimum essential equipment. We were good to go, so we continued our mission.

I was quiet for the rest of the flight, reflecting on what had happened and focusing on our mission. Our TACCO, Lt. Larry Anderson, was a prior-enlisted officer, so he was slightly older than the other junior officers and, therefore, more street-smart, which had earned him his callsign, "Jedi." Jedi noticed that the COTAC and SENSO were exchanging stories and using "colorful" language that he thought might make me uncomfortable, so he wrote down a note on his kneeboard to debrief the crew on "professional" communication in the cockpit.

When our mission that night was completed, it was time to land. Landing a jet on an aircraft carrier is difficult; landing a jet on an aircraft carrier at night is *really* difficult. Landing a jet on an aircraft carrier at night, with overcast skies blocking the horizon and still being shaken by almost dying during the takeoff, is ... well, it's one of the most difficult things I've had to do.

Carrier landing, night and day. Photo credit: Carl Vause

I was still new to the carrier aviation world and only had about 30 landings on an aircraft carrier by that point, 10 of which were night landings, and six of those 10 were on a moonlit night during training. I had a crew to get onboard safely, and everyone on the flight deck counted on me to do my job.

I came in for the first landing and had too much power on the jet, which is likely to happen when descending toward a small, dimly lit area knowing that you will hit it. You don't want to be underpowered! But my excess of power meant I sailed too far down the centerline; the tailhook on my jet slammed past all four arresting gear wires in the landing area, and we went flying again into the dark inky night sky. Missing all the arresting gears is called a "bolter."

As I slammed the throttles forward and rotated the nose up to climb away from the carrier and the water, I let my frustration get the best of me, and I uttered a string of profanities that would have made the saltiest of sailors blush. I used the F-word in every possible grammatical format—noun, verb, adverb, adjective, and conjunction. Upon hearing my reaction, Jedi quietly took a pen and scratched out his previous note about profanity.

I flew the landing pattern again to approach the carrier for another try. I had a better start but got underpowered, added too much power to compensate, and went around again. Aaagh!

Everyone on the ship, including my fellow aviators, was watching my struggle on the closed-circuit television screens all over the carrier.

Imagine what it's like to have 5,000 people watching you fail at your job.

My COTAC started talking to me in a smooth jazz voice. I couldn't let myself freak out. I didn't have that luxury.

We came back around a third time. I still struggled with getting the power right, but this time it was my ham-fisting of the control stick that resulted in me landing too flat and, therefore, the tailhook skipping over the number 4 arresting wire. Bolter number 3.

Thankfully, we had plenty of gas for these attempts, but by the third bolter, the pressure to land was at an all-time high, and I needed to get me and my crew onboard. Somehow, I managed to pull it together and landed on the fourth try. It never felt so good to be thrown forward against my torso harness as the tailhook caught the arresting gear. My legs shook as I taxied us out of the landing area and into our parking spot.

As I unstrapped from the ejection seat, I steeled myself for the judgment and criticism I was likely to receive for not being able to land the jet the first time. As one of the first women to fly in combat jets on this ship, I knew everything I did was scrutinized, and I felt like I had let down all the women who were on the carrier with me, trying to demonstrate that gender didn't matter in most roles in the military.

As I exited the jet, the aircrewman in the back, who had become less chatty the longer we flew in the landing pattern, patted me on the shoulder and exclaimed, "Don't worry, ma'am. I flew with someone who boltered five times." Then he added, with an encouraging smile, "And hey, thanks for the extra flight time!"

At the time, I was grateful for the encouragement. As I thought about his words later, it affected me much more deeply. Here was this kid...okay, he was probably 22, and I was about 27... and instead of running off the flight deck to get back to a warm, safe place or being angry at me for not getting onboard on the first try...he had stayed behind to make sure I was keeping my chin up. He was finding the joy in a situation where I could only find fear and self-doubt.

Maybe he had just seen too many Monty Python movies and couldn't get *"Always Look on the Bright Side of Life"* out of his head, but for me, his words were the beginning of a multi-year, personal journey to find joy in whatever I do.

* * *

It still blows my mind every time an airplane lifts off the ground. How can it be? How many times as children did we run along and jump into the air, hoping that we'd somehow defy gravity and stay airborne, but instead feel the disappointment of gravity pulling us back down to the ground? And yet, when we're in an airplane, at some point during the takeoff, the nose of the aircraft pulls up, and we magically lift into the air. I'm grateful to Bernoulli for figuring out fluid dynamics and to the Wright brothers for putting the principles to work to invent flight.

I've always loved things that aren't what they seemed to be. Airplanes certainly fit into that category. Who would ever look at a humongous C-5 Galaxy aircraft and imagine that weight lifting into the sky? Or that a round piece of vinyl could hold a symphony, or that a small block of metal, glass, and plastic could enable us to talk to one another across the world? I love human ingenuity. What other incredible things are yet to be discovered and created?

The word *flying* describes the feeling of weightlessness, transcending the downward pull of gravity and moving effortlessly through the sky. People on drug trips "fly" when they're "high." "I flew through that book" describes the ease and speed of reading.

Metaphorically, flying portrays freedom of movement and control of our destiny. But what's the science behind flight? It's time to geek out a little and talk about the four forces of flight, as the technical descriptions can help you understand how to take flight and soar in your own life.

The four forces of flight are thrust, weight, drag, and lift.

Thrust is what propels the aircraft forward. This is usually accomplished by an engine that turns a propeller or a jet engine that pushes air out behind the aircraft.

Propellors, or "props," are small airfoils carefully shaped to generate lift, yet instead of directing lift vertically like wings, props direct the lift horizontally, which pulls the airplane forward.

Jets generate propulsion by pulling in air, combining it with fuel, igniting the mixture, and using the resulting explosion to push the airplane forward.

Weight is the force caused by gravity, not only the physical weight and the aircraft's cargo.

Drag is the aerodynamic force that opposes the aircraft's motion forward through the air. An aircraft's wing is designed to be smooth to reduce drag.

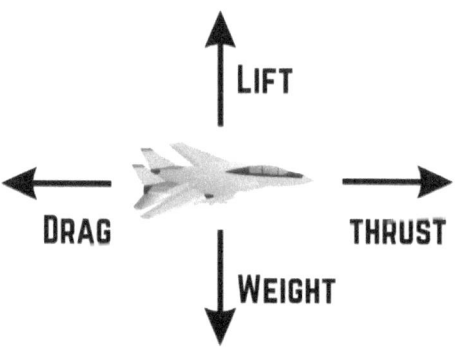

Lift is an upward force produced by the dynamic effect of the air acting on the airfoil. For an aircraft to rise into the air, a force must be created that exceeds the force of gravity. This force is called lift — like lots of little vacuum cleaners on top of the wing's surface, sucking the wing up into the air. That's lift!

Why am I asking you to read about aerodynamics? Because just as each of these forces affects an aircraft's ability to fly, the metaphoric representation of these four forces affects your ability to SOAR.

- **Thrust**: What motivates you internally to move forward in your life? What's important to you?
- **Weight**: What brings you down? How can you minimize the negative emotions in your life?
- **Drag**: What gets in your way and holds you back? How do you make your metaphorical "wing" smoother to reduce the drag in your life? One way is to quiet the voices in your head. Those inner critics are like little speed bumps on your wing that counteract the thrust in your life and slow down your progress. We'll talk more about inner critics in Chapter 2: Self-Awareness.
- **Lift**: How do you counteract the things that weigh you down? Lift comes from positive emotions like joy, gratitude, peace, and love. Who provides lift for you? What environments, activities, and moments are the ones that usually contribute to you feeling good?

Okay, now that you understand the basic concepts of how airplanes fly, I want to introduce another topic from aerodynamics that translates to being able to SOAR: stalls and spins. You know that to fly, an airplane must produce enough thrust to generate lift to overcome its weight and become airborne. When an airplane is flying and slows down too much such that the airflow over the lifting surface isn't enough to produce the required amount of lift, the aircraft stalls; if one of the wings stalls more deeply than the other, the aircraft spins.

Aircraft are designed to fly. Some airplanes are designed to be so stable that it takes a lot of pilot error to get them to spin.

When I went through Navy flight school, the first jet trainer I flew was the T-2C Buckeye, a two-seat jet designed to transition pilots from flying a propellor airplane to a faster jet-powered aircraft. The Buckeye was a fun aircraft and a great way to introduce a pilot to flying a jet. The affectionate nickname we gave it was the "Gerber Safety Jet" because it was a very stable platform, so much so that it was used to train us how to recover from stalls and spins.

I loved doing stalls and spin training. I had a strong stomach for aerobatics. It was fun to put the aircraft into "uncontrolled flight," having memorized the procedures to recover and fly smoothly again.

Not all aircraft are designed to be as stable as the T-2C, but all are designed to fly. Assuming there's enough altitude, a pilot can sometimes recover from uncontrolled flight by letting go of the controls and allowing the plane to do what it was designed to do. When an airplane is about to stall, you can physically feel the airplane shake as the air over the wings becomes disrupted. The shaking is known as "buffet." If I'm flying close to stall speed, feeling the buffet, I simply let go of the control stick, allowing the nose of the aircraft to drop. It will nose down, speed up, and I can fly it again. If I don't release the pressure and let it continue to a stall, the nose will snap down more sharply, and I'll lose more altitude in the recovery, but the aircraft will still seek to recover and fly.

I want to clarify that I'm talking about a simplified version of stall dynamics to illustrate a metaphorical point, so all you Reddit r/aviation bubbas, relax.

Let's bring this metaphor home. What I've found in my life is that when I grip too tightly to my expectations about how my life should play out, or I try to exert too much control over outcomes (and people!), I often find myself getting into that turbulent state of buffet and, sometimes, "stalling," where my life feels like it's taking a dramatic downturn. When I loosen my grip on my expectations and allow myself to be open to possibilities, my life feels like it's returning to normal flight.

When something doesn't turn out the way I wanted it to, I remind myself to release my grip on outcomes and trust that there's a reason why my life is unfolding as it is. I am designed to SOAR if I allow myself to do so.

Your Flight Plan

1. What activity — personal or business — makes you soar?
2. How do you feel when you soar?
3. How do you express soaring?
4. How would you feel if you could bring that feeling to all aspects of your life?

"If you want to fly, you have to give up
what weighs you down."

—ROY T. BENNETT

Chapter 2

SELF-AWARENESS

"Tell me, what is it you plan to do with your one wild and precious life?"

—MARY OLIVER

The S in SOAR stands for self-awareness. This might seem obvious. Of course, we must be aware of who we are and what we do in the world. But in what level of awareness are you living? Are you honoring your values in the way you show up in the world? Have you taken the time to reflect on what you want your purpose to be? Do you know what your values and life vision are?

Don't worry if you don't; most of us don't take the time to reflect on why we're on this planet. We're just surviving. Now and then, that nagging question — why am I here? — pops up into our consciousness. For me, it happens when someone I care about dies. When I'm reminded that this life is finite, that there are no do-overs, that if I don't live the life I want now, I can't count on there being a tomorrow in which to live it, I am brought back to extreme self-awareness of how I need to live my life — one that honors my values and is in keeping with my life vision.

I do not spend every moment of every day thinking, *Is what I'm doing right now honoring my values?* It's not like I'm pouring myself a cup of coffee and wondering if this beverage honors my values. But I do check in with myself regularly about it. And when I'm having those moments of fear, wondering if things are going to work out or of regret, worrying if I made the wrong decision, I check in with myself and remind myself that as long as I'm living a life that honors my values, I'm going to be fine.

Do you have moments of catastrophic thinking when imagining what might happen in your future, and your default is to go to the worst-case scenarios? I used to do this often because I'm a planner and want to feel ready for every possible contingency. I blame my pilot training and Virgo-ness for this need to feel like I'm always in control. What's interesting is how much mental energy I put toward expecting the worst-case scenarios rather than being prepared for them.

Here's what I mean: Let's say you look at the weather forecast, and it says it's going to rain this weekend, and you have made plans for a hike with a friend. At this moment, you could get upset and think, *Geez, why does it always have to rain on the weekend when you want to be outside and not during the week when you're inside working? And now, what are we going to do?* You'd been looking forward to this hike and the time with your friend, and now the stupid weather will ruin it.

At that moment, you have a choice. You could go down that path of being pissed off about something that hasn't happened yet (rain during your planned hike), or you could note that you might need to make an alternate plan with your friend.

I chuckle at this scenario because we pilots call meteorologists "weather guessers" for a reason. They're making their best forecast based on weather patterns and lots of data, but they never know with 100 percent probability what ol' Mother Nature will do. So why get mad about something that hasn't happened yet? There's a good chance that by the time you get to the weekend, it won't rain at the exact time you want to hike, and you will have been pissed off for nothing. Of course, it might rain, but why not wait to see if there's actually something to be pissed off about? And if you made an alternate plan, there's no need.

The point of this example is that we don't know exactly what will happen in the future, so why would you want to create and experience negative emotions for situations that haven't happened yet? If you are like me and you're going to fantasize about what might happen, why not fantasize about something positive? This is often called "visualizing": imagining yourself getting what you want.

I used to engage in a lot of catastrophic thinking when I was flying in the Navy. Many nights, I laid in my rack underneath the number two catapult and wondered what I would do if I lost my brakes while taxiing on the flight deck? The official procedure was to lower your tailhook; the unofficial procedure was to signal frantically to the ground crew by pointing back at the wheels with a thumbs down. I imagined doing this, and then I'd imagine no one would react in time, and the ship would turn, and we'd go sliding over the side of the deck into the ocean with our ejection seats unarmed.

After a few nights of crappy sleep, I had to check myself and resist the temptation to go down this mental path of fearing the worst. If we call fun fantasizing daydreaming, maybe this was day-nightmaring? I allowed myself the "what if" situation, but once I completed the mandatory emergency steps in my head, I told myself, *Relax, you're in your stateroom, and it's time to go to sleep, so start counting sheep instead.*

When a concern came up, I imagined the worst-case scenario, I'd think of a plan to mitigate it, and then I'd move on to the next thing. So, worry, then fix the worry.

Years later, in my corporate career, when I didn't have to worry anymore about physical survival, I realized that these fears in my head were not serving me. I didn't have an emergency checklist to memorize for catastrophic workplace failures. Instead, most of the scenarios popping up in my head were things like, "If I say this in the meeting, I'll sound stupid," or "If I don't impress my VP, I'll never get promoted," or "If I don't spend every waking moment thinking about work, someone else will, and they'll get my job." Lots of catastrophic thinking was all in my head. Rather than noting the thought and fixing it, I fantasized about transforming it into something positive. For example, instead of thinking, "If I say this in the meeting, I'll sound stupid," I began imagining myself speaking up and people liking what I said. I stopped worrying about impressing my VP and instead focused on enjoying my work.

As a coach, when my clients say, "What if I completely blow this?" I love to ask them, "What if you don't? What if you're wildly successful?" This is such a powerful question because we're so conditioned to prepare for (and expect!) the worst.

It's not our fault, by the way. We have catastrophic thinking to thank for the fact that we are still living on this planet. Catastrophic thinking has kept (most)[3] humans from doing stupid things that get us killed, and thus our species has survived. Unfortunately, our world has evolved faster than our fear instinct, and we still hold back from taking risks that could be incredibly beneficial to us. Often, it takes a big shakeup to highlight how we've been holding back and not living the fulfilling lives we deserve.

We tend to get back in touch with what's most important to us when we experience challenging times, like losing a loved one. There were two times when I felt like my world was falling

---

3 A moment of silence for the recipients of The Darwin Awards (https://darwinawards.com/darwin/), which "salute the improvement of the human genome by honoring those who accidentally remove themselves from it in a spectacular manner."

apart, forcing me to check in with myself about what I wanted in my life.

The first time was during my flight training in the Navy. I had performed well enough in flight school to earn a spot in a squadron that flew the FA-18 A/B Hornet in a support role (this was before women were allowed to fly in combat squadrons). The 1991 Tailhook scandal had happened about a year before I was a student at the Hornet training squadron, aka the Fleet Replacement Squadron, or FRS. I was the first woman to go straight into the Hornet FRS; the few other women who had flown Hornets had transitioned from a fleet squadron, flown a different jet, or had been instructors in the training command, racking up flight hours that would better prepare them for the rigors of learning to fly a new aircraft.

Walking into the Hornet FRS was like walking into a den of pit vipers waiting to strike. I remember walking down the passageway and saying a cheerful, "Good morning, sir!" to one of the instructors and getting no response, only an icy stare. The ready room, where students and instructors hung out between our flights, would go silent when I walked in. This was shocking to me. I loved spending time in the ready room in my previous training squadron because you'd learn from other students and instructors, listening to them talk about their flights. Plus, naval aviators have robust senses of humor, so it was always a fun place to spend time.

At the FRS, I started avoiding the ready room because it was clear my presence was not welcomed. As I described in my book, *She's Just Another Navy Pilot*, the second-in-command at the FRS posted an article in the ready room about why women shouldn't be allowed to fly in combat. When I asked if the ready room bulletin board was a place to post opinion pieces and if I could share one, rumors started that I'd demanded to have the previous article taken down and mine put up. Despite receiving minimal instruction during my flights with the instructor pilots, I completed the training and spent the next year flying Hornets at VAQ-34 without any issues.

The single-seat, F/A-18A at VAQ-34. We also flew the two-seat version, the F/A-18B.

Around the same time, the ban on women flying in combat aviation was lifted, and decision-makers in Washington, DC, were determining which women would go to which combat squadrons. I'd hoped to stay flying the F/A-18 Hornet, but I had friends in DC who let me know that one of the senior instructors at the Hornet training squadron told the decision-makers that the instructors didn't want me to come back because I had been a troublemaker and they didn't want to deal with me. To them, a woman standing up for herself is labeled a troublemaker. I was disappointed not to continue flying Hornets, as I already had accumulated over 130 flight hours in the aircraft, and I loved flying the F/A-18; it felt like being behind the controls of the most amazing video game ever.

The skipper of VAQ-34 got the news about where all the women aviators in his squadron would be transferred while I was on a cross-country flight to San Diego, supporting a missile exercise. I'll never forget calling my skipper on a pay phone and his hesitation about telling me that I would be transferred to San Diego to fly S-3B Vikings.

The S-3B Viking. Not as sexy as a fighter, but it's still a jet. Photo credit: Kathleen Spane

I was devastated, not because I had anything against flying S-3s, but because it felt like I had never been given a fair chance at the FRS. I was engaged to be married to another Hornet pilot and taking the S-3 orders would mean moving to San Diego and living over 300 miles away from him for the next three to four years.

I had a decision to make; I could refuse the orders and serve in a staff (non-flying) job until the next assignment of women to combat squadrons the following year and hope that the previous posse of Hornet FRS instructors had moved on and I'd be given a slot in F/A-18s. This was not a given, and there was a strong chance I'd get refused again, but at least I'd be on the same base as my soon-to-be (and future ex-) husband. Or I could accept my orders and be one of the first women to fly in a combat squadron on the first West Coast aircraft carrier deployment with women onboard.

This was obviously a major decision. I had to take stock of what mattered most to me then. I valued teamwork, adventure, purpose, and leadership. I have a strong sense of patriotism and service. I felt I'd have more impact by being one of the first women combat aviators deployed on an aircraft carrier with women integrated. As an officer, I could be a strong role model for all the sailors, not just the women, and for my fellow aviators, I'd be part of their team. My experience at the F/A-18 FRS indicated that I would have challenges being accepted as part of that team. I didn't know if the S-3 community would be more open, but the opportunity to be a pioneer felt like a big responsibility and one I felt confident I could handle. I'll discuss what happened at the S-3 FRS in Chapter 5, Responsibility.

By the way, another woman received the same orders I did. She made a different decision — to wait — and the following cycle, she received orders to fly the Hornet. She went on to become the first woman to command a carrier air wing and is now a three-star admiral.

Could that have been me? Maybe. I don't spend time imagining what could have been because it isn't, and it feels like a waste of mental energy to do that thought exercise. Do I regret my decision? Not at all.

My second major inflection point was when my marriage fell apart. It had been struggling for years. I talk about it as a third entity because I think that's how it should be treated. There are two people, and the relationship between them. The two people determine what that relationship is and how they want it to exist in the world, and then they make decisions that have an effect (positive/negative/neutral) on the relationship as if it were a third "person," separate from the two people involved.

We started having serious challenges in our marriage after only a couple of years. Because we were both in the military, we hadn't spent much time together, and once we did, we struggled with our different perspectives on what a relationship should be and how to be with each other. We came very close to getting a divorce after five years of marriage, but we decided we didn't want to give up yet and instead went to graduate school together.

After graduating from business school, we started our careers in Silicon Valley and were blessed with two beautiful children – our son and our daughter.

Unfortunately, our marriage was not as healthy as it looked from the outside. I own my part in failing to support the relationship, and it took me years to do so. I didn't stand up for myself enough and for what I needed. Instead, I blamed my ex-husband for not giving me what I wanted, even though perhaps I didn't communicate it strongly enough. I felt unappreciated and taken for granted. I'm not saying he didn't appreciate me; I'm saying that's how I felt. Over the years, my resentment toward him grew.

I decided to engage in an emotional affair with someone I worked with. It was an easy way out, and I fell for it. He was also struggling in his marriage and coming together for support felt right at the time. Neither of us was in the right headspace to start a relationship — certainly not while we were still married to other people — and needless to say, that relationship didn't last either.

I could stop here and say I had two failed relationships at that point, but what is *failure*? Simply put, it's "the lack of success." But then, what is *success*? Does a relationship have to last forever to be successful? You probably know people in unhappy marriages that have lasted years: Are they successful relationships?

I like to think of the word *fail* as an acronym: First Attempt In Learning: FAIL. I'd only been in one serious relationship before the one with my ex-husband, which lasted just six months. I didn't know it then, but I didn't appreciate what it meant to be in a romantic relationship with someone. I hadn't learned how to be a good partner.

Instead of taking some time to be alone and learn more about myself and what I wanted, I jumped from short-term relationship to short-term relationship until I jumped into dating my now ex-husband.

There were warning signs before we got married, but I ignored them because I was doing what I thought I should: get married before you're too old to have children. I was unknowingly jumping the gun: I was 26 when I got married and didn't have my two children until I was 34 and 36, so in hindsight, I could have waited, but at the time, I didn't know that.

So, divorced and heartbroken, I embarked on a journey to understand who I was and what I wanted. I went through a lot of therapy (weekly when I was going through the divorce and the affair) and read A LOT of self-help books (see Resources for the ones I recommend). I went through programs like Landmark

Education. I volunteered. I prayed. I started practicing yoga and learned how to meditate. I deeply reflected on what I was doing with my one wild and precious life, as the poet Mary Oliver calls our earthly existence in her beautiful poem "The Summer Day."

As part of my roles at Google and Facebook, I was allowed to have a few sessions with coaches. They asked me uncomfortable questions like, "What do you want?" Such a simple question and yet often difficult to answer. They encouraged me to think beyond my job and more about my life. It opened my mind to think about what my "dream life" would be. I realized that creativity and art were important to me, but I had stuffed these things away when I entered the Navy. There's a group mindset in naval aviation about what behavior is acceptable (teamwork, physical risk, drinking) and what isn't (anything feminine, including art!). I'd also been raised with some negative attitudes toward artists, so I'd never considered becoming one.

My experience as a coaching client empowered me to reconsider what success and failure were. I learned that when you hear, "It's your life; you gotta live it the way you want," it means the way YOU want, not what society is telling you, or your parents, or your friends, or your spouse. But first, you need to figure out what *you* want and what's important to you.

When I flew in the Navy, a few things motivated me. First, I have to admit, was making my parents proud. I also felt a strong sense of duty to my country and wanted to protect our democracy by serving in the military.

I also felt a responsibility to prove that women were capable of more than we were getting credit for at the time I served — the '90s. Despite not being allowed to serve in combat units, women fought and died in Desert Storm in 1991. Later that year, we had the Tailhook '91 scandal and the Clarence Thomas Supreme

Court confirmation hearings, when Anita Hill was standing up for women who had been sexually harassed. America was questioning the role of women — how we should be treated and what jobs we are capable of performing.

Finding My True Self at Goldman Sachs

As a second-year business school student, I thought I should explore possibilities and try something new.

One of my best friends at Wharton loved her internship at Goldman Sachs, the top investment banking firm.

I went to the interview for the prestige. While I thought I would learn a lot and the work would be interesting, I mostly did this because it would look great on my resume. And, oh yes, they paid a shit ton of money... If you're taking notes on how to be self-aware, these are the wrong reasons to go to on an interview or take any job unless you value prestige and wealth. BTW, it's totally fine if those are your values. There is no judgment on values; they are as individual as your fingerprint because they're based on who you are and the life experiences that have shaped you. Anyway, back to GS...

The interviewer saw right through me. He asked me the stereotypical question: "Why is a dollar in my hand today worth more than a dollar tomorrow?" My friend prepared me for this question, and I responded with my somewhat canned answer. Well, this is Goldman Sachs. They knew I'd know the canned answer, so the interviewer asked me a deeper question about the time value of money that quickly revealed that I had no idea what the f--- I was talking about.

He looked at me and asked, "You don't really want to be an investment banker, do you?"

I looked at him, hesitated, and stuttered as I tried to justify why I was there. Then I finally honored my integrity. I sighed and said, "No, I don't."

I was embarrassed. But I learned a lesson. Knowing what's important to you and what type of day-to-day life you want to have is critical. I like money as much as anyone, but it's not one of my top values. For some people (like investment bankers who love being investment bankers!), it is, and that's cool... everyone is different. But know who you are.

I was several years older than most of my business school classmates, and I didn't want to spend 100 to 120 hours a week in an office and travel all the time. I had done that for the past 10 years in the Navy. One of the reasons I left the Navy was that I wanted to have children, and I didn't want to deploy as a parent. I greatly respect parents who do it, but I didn't want it for myself. Investment banking was the right job for my best friend and the wrong job for me. Have you ever been in an interview and said, "This sucks. But I need the job, so I'll play the game?" If so, I give you points for self-awareness. And I hope you had the courage to walk out of the interview.

I eventually realized that to soar, I needed to follow my own path.

Strengths and Values: Be True to Yourself

How do you know what your path is? You can start by knowing your strengths and values. Employing your strengths and honoring your values enables you to make better choices when you come to forks in your life — what roles you take on in work and life and with whom you surround yourself. If you don't know who you are and what's important to you, then you are in danger of spending too much time in the wrong role with the wrong people in the wrong place…for you. Again, we all have our unique combination of strengths and values. What might be a horrible fit for me is a perfect fit for you.

I chose a few jobs that weren't right for me because I felt like I had to have a job and make money or because the company sounded cool. What inevitably would happen is that the novelty of a new company would wear off after a year or so, and I'd see that the job wasn't a good fit for my strengths or that the company wasn't aligned with my values.

Strengths: What you're good at doing and what you love to do.

Notice that definition: "What you're good at doing AND what you love to do." It's not an "or."

Too many people think their strengths are the things they're good at doing, whether or not they enjoy doing them. They don't recognize the importance of *joy* in the work they do.

One of the best ways to identify your strengths is to take the Gallup Company's Strengthsfinder Assessment online. It will help you identify your top five strengths, and they provide a ton of excellent content to help you think about how those strengths can be leveraged in various jobs.

If you don't want to buy the assessment (although I *highly* recommend it; it's worth the 20 dollars), you can open a document online or take a sheet of paper and write "Love it" on the top left and "Loathe It" on the top right. Throughout your week, note the various activities you're doing and put them in the column on the left if you love doing that activity, or write it in the column on the right if you're neutral or don't really care for it. This will give you an idea of things you love to do; next, you need to assess whether or not you're good at each one.

What Are Your Values?

Think of values as the set of fingerprints that are unique to you in how you want to live *your* life. Not how your parents/spouse/friends/family think you should live it, but how *you* want to live it.

Values are the qualities of life you are drawn to, which are important to you.

They can be "lofty" values, like:

Love	Patience	Diversity	Fairness
Caring	Compassion	Leadership	Integrity

They can be aspirations that are sometimes judged by others as "less-lofty" ways to guide your life:

Wealth	Fun	Leisure	Risk-taking

Don't let society dictate what your values "should" be. "Should" is a word that detours so many of us from living fulfilling lives. Have you heard of that saying, "Don't 'should' all over yourself?" It makes me smile, not only because of the play on words but also because we're so conditioned to want to be liked and accepted. There's nothing wrong with wanting to be liked — it's human nature, after all — but sacrificing your values to be liked is, at a minimum, setting yourself up for resentment and disappointment and, worse, losing yourself and what's important to you in a pursuit to please other people.

You can give your values names to summarize something meaningful to you. In my work with clients, they've identified values like:

- Sparkle: feeling beautiful, full of life and light
- Wolf: self-sufficiency, yet part of a pack
- Cloud: Sensitive, flexible, and dynamic

Your values are yours. They are what's most important to you in how you live your life. My values are service, family, humor, curiosity, gratitude, and creativity. How do these values show up in my life? When I have a choice to make, I can lean on them to assist me.

Before you go through a list of values and highlight which ones might sound good, you can ask yourself some questions to get into the mindset —or even better, the *feeling* — of how you want to live your life:

- What's a perfect day for me?
- If I had a million dollars to give away, who would I give it to?
- What qualities do I appreciate in others?
- What makes me mad? (these are times when your values are being stepped on)
- If I had six months to live, what would I do?
- If money were no object, what would I do?

Okay, now that you're picturing your ideal life (and why shouldn't you be aiming for the life you love?), it's time to zero in on your unique values. Here are four exercises:

1. Think of a peak experience in your life. It doesn't necessarily need to be an extremely joyful one, but it should be a time in your life when you felt like you were in the "flow," or dare I say, "soaring"? You felt in the groove like what you were doing mattered, and you felt fulfilled. Close your eyes and put yourself back in this experience. Engage as many senses

as possible — what do you see? What can you hear around you in this experience? Can you notice any smells? Are your taste buds involved? Are you touching anything? Relive the experience and notice what values are coming up for you as being a part of this experience.

For example, if a project at work went exceptionally well, what was it about the project? Was it light-hearted and fun? Were the people involved serious and driven? Was it mathematically challenging, or did it involve more "right-brain" creative thinking? Notice what made an impression on you about this experience.

2. Conversely, reflect on a time when you felt really low and stuck. If it was a work experience, were you dreading Mondays and couldn't wait for Friday? No matter the setting or situation, tap back into that feeling that's the opposite of "flow." Maybe you felt disrespected, unappreciated, or uncomfortable... name the negative emotions. Go through a similar exercise as in the previous peak experience, and mentally place yourself back in the situation as much as possible without reigniting any trauma. Feel what it's like to be in this place of being deeply unsatisfied and note which values might be dishonored in this situation.

3. Imagine yourself at a party for your 100th birthday many years in the future. People from all the various phases of your life are coming to celebrate you. The partygoers aren't only friends and family; they are people who have interacted with you over the years. Each one is handing you a birthday card with a lovely note inside, describing your impact on them. What do the cards say?

4. Ask your friends and family for the three words that best describe your "superpowers" — your strongest, best qualities. Reach out to as many people as possible. You can tell them

you're doing some "inner work" or "self-discovery" or reading this wonderful book about how to SOAR, and you're just curious. Ask them what they believe are your three best, strongest qualities — what they come to you for or where they see you offering substantial value to others. The superpowers won't necessarily translate directly to "values," but they will give you insight into how your values are showing up in the qualities you're known for among the people in your life, which will provide insight into what is most important for you.

Now that you've done these exercises and taken some time for self-reflection, it's time to put these thoughts into words so you can actively honor your values.

Below is a list of values from Brené Brown's book *Daring to Lead* to help you identify what's most important in your life. Feel free to use your own descriptors (like the ones mentioned above — Sparkle, Wolf, Cloud) to express your unique values.

Accountability	Collaboration	Dignity
Achievement	Commitment	Diversity
Adaptability	Community	Environment
Adventure	Compassion	Efficiency
Altruism	Competence	Equality
Ambition	Confidence	Ethics
Authenticity	Connection	Excellence
Balance	Contentment	Fairness
Beauty	Contribution	Faith
Being the best	Cooperation	Family
Belonging	Courage	Financial stability
Career	Creativity	Forgiveness
Caring	Curiosity	Freedom

Friendship
Fun
Future generations
Generosity
Giving back
Grace
Gratitude
Growth
Harmony
Health
Home
Honesty
Hope
Humility
Humor
Inclusion
Independence
Initiative
Integrity
Intuition
Job security
Joy
Justice
Kindness
Knowledge
Leadership
Learning

Legacy
Leisure
Love
Loyalty
Making a difference
Nature
Openness
Optimism
Order
Parenting
Patience
Patriotism
Peace
Perseverance
Personal fulfillment
Power
Pride
Recognition
Reliability
Resourcefulness
Respect
Responsibility
Risk-taking
Safety
Security
Self-discipline
Self-expression

Self-respect
Serenity
Service
Simplicity
Spirituality
Sportsmanship
Stewardship
Success
Teamwork
Thrift
Time
Tradition
Travel
Trust
Truth
Understanding
Uniqueness
Usefulness
Vision
Vulnerability
Wealth
Well-being
Wholeheartedness
Wisdom
Write your own

I recommend using this list to highlight the values important to you, then refining that list down to the three to five values that stand out the most. If you find more than 10 on this list that resonate with you, write each one down on a Post-it Note, and then rank them: Compare two at a time and decide which one matters most to you.

For example, if you're comparing honesty and freedom, and you decide freedom is more important to you, then put freedom on top and honesty beneath it. When you look at the next value you chose from the list, let's say it's community, you compare community to freedom and decide which one matters more to you.

Keep doing this until you've ranked them all, then narrow your values down to the top three to five. I have six, so I don't feel you must have an exact number. These are *your* values. But try to focus on getting to the most important, highest-value values.

* * *

"Every time I was called on in class, I was sure that I
was about to embarrass myself. Every time I took a test,
I was sure that it had gone badly. And every time I didn't
embarrass myself — or even excelled — I believed that
I had fooled everyone yet again. One day soon, the jig
would be up."

—SHERYL SANDBERG

The Great Imposter: Doubting Our Self-Awareness

Why do we talk ourselves out of applying for the right job at the right company, asking for the right salary and benefits? Why does that internal, infernal voice say, "You are not good enough, and sooner or later, everyone here will figure out you're not smart enough to be here?" That feeling has been referred to as "Imposter Syndrome."

I don't like this term, and I debated whether I should even include it in my book because it feels like it's mostly been used to describe women's internal struggles with feeling qualified and whether or not we're "enough." The term "imposter" feels like it's perpetuating systemic undervaluing of women's contributions, that women don't belong in the successful ranks of the world.

Instead of "imposter syndrome," I will coin my own term, FONBE: Fear of Not Being Enough. This fear shows up in almost all of us, regardless of our gender identity, and it doesn't insinuate in its name that a group of people doesn't belong.

FONBE, FKA Imposter syndrome, can be defined as a collection of feelings of inadequacy that persist despite evident success.[4] Oddly, people who suffer from this often are the high achievers, as they tend to set higher expectations for themselves.

Having a strong sense of self can minimize the feelings of FONBE. Knowing our strengths and what matters most to us in our lives enables us to figure things out in situations where we're not sure what to do. Rather than fearing we're not enough and someone else will notice, we can step into a place of commitment and show up as willing learners (more on this in the next chapter, "Open").

Your So-Called Weakness Might Be Your Strength

After realizing that investment banking was not for me, I was hired at Bain and Company, and I experienced major FONBE because my coworkers had been on Wall Street or had been consulting for a few years. I was older than all the other consultants because

---

4 From Harvard Business Review article "Overcoming Imposter Syndrome" by Gill Corkindale, HBR.org May 7, 2008

I had spent 10 years in the military. I was as old as, if not older, than most of the managers who were managing me.

I was very intimidated. I should have realized this was a normal reaction, even for the former consultants and investment bankers in my class.

I opened up to my manager about my fears. I said, "You're asking me to talk to people who have been in business for twice as long as I was in the Navy. And yet I'm expected to go in and tell them how to improve their business."

He said, "Think of it this way. Management consultants are like business doctors. You see a new patient. The patient's going to know the particulars of their unique situations. And every company will be different and have different issues.

"But you can look across all of those companies — just like a doctor looks across a bunch of patients — and understand how a disease or condition might affect them. Then you work with that patient to understand how to improve their unique individual situation. Your 10 years in the military combined with the education and experience in your MBA program were your 'medical school.' Now you get to go work with corporate patients."

That helped me realize the unique value I bring.

This leader reminded me of my worth. Good leaders do that. No one has my unique experience: Mathematics major, Navy pilot, Wharton grad, creative artist, author. That's why they hired me. That's why I was there. They did not hire me because they expected me to provide the same kind of input as a male Wall Street banker. They expected me to question things differently and to add my unique expertise. Once I realized that I had a lot to offer, I was able to be a better-contributing member of the team. Keeping that perspective was still sometimes a challenge; after all, I am human!

Have you ever wondered if you belonged? That's normal. It is quite possible that we don't realize we have talents that we take for granted. But those might be talents that the world values highly. Maybe you can speak in front of an audience. Lots of people can't! Maybe you can write a blog post in two minutes flat. Many people can't do that! What is your superpower?

Although I was working with companies where I did not know much about their industry, I had skills from business school and management skills from the military that could help.

I put a lot of pressure on myself because I felt I must come up with the perfect answer for these clients. As I began to realize my issues with FONBE, I realized I was adding value by bringing my unique perspective and combining it with the views of other people on my team. As a result, we could present a wider range of options for a client.

When you see the value in your experience, you can overcome those feelings of inadequacy and fear of not being enough as I did.

You Know More Than You Think

Are you a fellow fan of the television series *The Simpsons*? Do you recall the episode when Bart was an exchange student in Algeria?

He has no idea how to speak French with the locals. He's being put to work by two guys who are using him as free slave labor for weeks, and he's complaining. "Oh my gosh, I can't believe it, how did this happen to me?" Then he's walking down the street, and he's reviewing the whole situation in his head and having his pity party. All of a sudden, his thoughts are in French, and he is speaking out loud in French. He stops and says, "I can't believe it." Actually, he says, *"Incroyable!"*

I love that story because he didn't realize that during the weeks of living in Algeria, he was soaking up the language and it was germinating in his brain. Have you ever sat in a meeting and had a thought but didn't say it because you were afraid it might not be well-received? Then a coworker says the same thing you're thinking, and she's congratulated for being brilliant? You know more than you think.

Decisions and Consequences

A quick side note about decisions: IMHO, there are no bad decisions. There are choices and consequences. I've learned to stop getting so wound up about making the right decision and instead make a decision that feels like the best one for me and then make sure that I make that decision right.

Being self-aware and knowing what's most important to you enables you to have more confidence in the decisions you make.

Besides looking like a messed-up mammogram, this illustration is a great example of decisions and possibilities. We make choices every day in how we want to live our life: who we want to spend time with, what we do for work, how we want to see the world. Granted, where you're born affects many of the choices that are available to you and where your life path will take you. But you still have the responsibility to choose (more on this in Chapter 5 Responsibility). And once you've made the decision, it's done. The black lines above represent the past: paths that you could have taken by choices you could have made but didn't. You can never go back to that same decision point because it's in the past. We spend too much time thinking about the past — a figment of our imagination. The past is not reality. Today, now, is reality. Even the future isn't reality, but at least

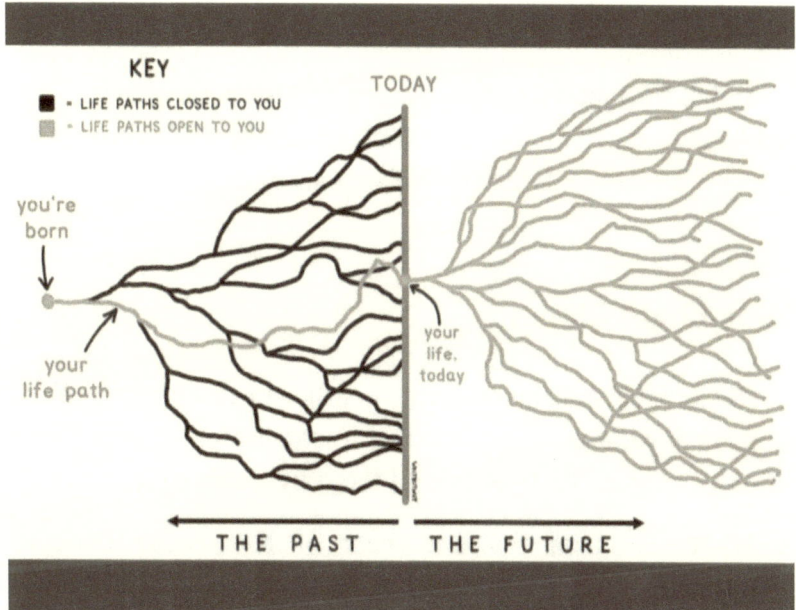

KEY
■ - LIFE PATHS CLOSED TO YOU
▦ - LIFE PATHS OPEN TO YOU

TODAY

you're
born

your
life path

your
life,
today

THE PAST   THE FUTURE

Illustration used with permission from Tim Urban / Wait But Why

our choices today can shape it, unlike the past, which is done and unchangeable.

* * *

In conclusion, self-awareness is critical if you want to SOAR. You need to know what kind of airplane you're flying. By reflecting on your strengths and values, you'll have a clearer sense of what makes you tick and what matters most to you in this world we live in. Be honest with yourself about this.

I think Steve Jobs said it best when he was addressing the 2005 graduating class at Stanford University:

"Your time is limited, so don't waste it living someone else's life. Don't be trapped by dogma — which is living with the results of other people's thinking. Don't let the noise of other's opinions drown out your own inner voice. And most important, have the courage to follow your heart and intuition. They somehow already know what you truly want to become. Everything else is secondary."[5]

Your Flight Plan

1. Review the values you created earlier in this chapter. Write them down somewhere or create a screensaver for your phone so you can remind yourself of these frequently. Get creative!

2. What aspect of FONBE (Fear of Not Being Enough) resonates with you? How can you reframe that perceived weakness and turn it into a strength? Ask yourself, "Because I have/am (*perceived weakness*), I can do *something* better." Or "Because I am the only _____, I can provide a unique perspective." For example, because I am the youngest person on the staff, I provide the Gen Z view that is important to consider.

3. Know your strengths and check in with yourself regularly. Are you in a role and doing work that is leveraging your strengths?

4. Make the time to get in touch with who you are and what's important for you in life. If you were to die in a month, would you be able to look back at the previous 30 days and be satisfied with how you spent your time? You can start by looking at the personal values and strengths you determined

---

5 "'You've got to find what you love,' Jobs says," June 12, 2005, *Stanford News*, https://news.stanford.edu/2005/06/12/youve-got-find-love-jobs-says/.

in this chapter and note what brings you joy in your life. You can also check out some of the books I recommend in Resources. I've read so many books over the past 30 years that I could open my own self-help bookstore in my living room. If you're like me and feel that buying (and sometimes, reading-ha!) books about a topic I'm interested in somehow makes me more likely to know how to do the thing, like knowledge through purchasing-osmosis, then knock yourself out. Check these books out at your local library before you build up a massive bookshelf of self-help books and see which ones resonate with you.

"You will only ever have two choices, love or fear. Choose love, and don't ever let fear turn you against your playful heart."

—JIM CARREY

Chapter 3

OPENNESS

"We live in a wonderful world that is full of beauty, charm, and adventure. There is no end to the adventures that we can have if only we seek them with our eyes open."

—JAWAHARLAL NEHRU

In the previous chapter, I described the decision I had to make about whether to accept my orders to fly the S-3B Viking or fight to remain in the F/A-18 Hornet community. Because I was self-aware of what was most important to me, I decided to accept the orders. Part of my self-awareness was being open to a possibility that wasn't the one I had planned on or originally wanted.

After I joined the S-3 community and deployed to the Persian Gulf, I had to be open to learning from pilots who had a lot to teach me but had a brusque and direct communication style that rubbed many people the wrong way. I'm referring to the senior landing signal officers, or LSOs: the experienced pilots who grade every carrier landing.

As I've mentioned, landing on an aircraft carrier is an exercise fraught with danger, so the job of the LSO was introduced almost immediately after carrier aviation came into being in the 1920s to assist naval aviators with landing safely. The senior LSOs on my first deployment were extremely demanding and not at all delicate in conveying their high standards.

As a female pilot on my first carrier deployment, it would have been easy to assume that they were taking their frustrations about the integration out on me and giving me lower grades than I might deserve. However, I had to be open to the possibility that as a first-tour aviator, I still had a lot to learn about landing well on a carrier, and as much as I didn't like these particular pilots, they had a lot to teach me, if I could keep an open mind about it.

Thankfully, one of the experienced LSOs in my squadron whom I trusted, Lt. Joe "Flojo" Keith, convinced me that I was making normal first-tour aviator mistakes, and that's why my grades weren't as good as I wanted them to be; not because the senior LSOs were out to "get the women." Flojo advised me that my landings would improve if I listened to the senior LSOs' feedback and did my homework. I stayed open, I listened, I did the work, and I got better.

* * *

When I worked at Facebook (now Meta), the people on my team had the title of content writer. In other companies I had been at, including Google, that role was titled content strategist, which is perceived as providing more value because the role requires strategic thinking and cross-functional collaboration beyond the sole act of writing the content. Content strategists determine how to use content to explain a product better and work with product teams to help make improvements.

My team was growing to support the increased number of products being released, and I felt we'd get more qualified people to apply for our jobs if their title better reflected their work, which was content strategy.

I began a campaign to change their title. In a large, public company like Meta, you can't just decide to call your role something else. Many departments weigh in, including legal but especially the People Operations team (also known as human resources in many companies). I began contacting cross-functional partners to explain why we needed to change the job title.

I was on the business side of Facebook. The head of the consumer content strategy team was a couple of levels senior to me. Other people I worked with on the business side told me she and her team were very protective of their titles, and they didn't want anyone else in the company to have the same ones.

That immediately rubbed me the wrong way. No one organization, I felt, had the right to say only their team can be called content strategists. It would be like an engineering team saying only the engineers in their organization could be called "engineers." I put together a presentation and laid out a case for why the people on my team should be called content strategists. I scheduled time with her to present my recommendation, which to me was airtight. The people on my team were doing content strategy work, we needed to grow our team, and we needed the best candidates, so therefore, we needed to change their titles.

She disagreed. I tried to convince her rather than get curious about her resistance. We tried to work it out, but it was a nonstarter for her.

I found out later that she had fought tooth and nail to ensure content strategists were included in product discussions. Too often, content and design are an afterthought when a product team is creating or updating products. For me to come to her and tell her I wanted to change my team's name to content strategist, felt like one more battle she had to fight in defense of her team. I respected that, and I wish I had known that history, but I didn't really ask, and she didn't share it then. If I had explored that conversation with her with an open, inquisitive, relationship-building approach, I think we both would have walked away from the conversation feeling heard by the other and more willing to collaborate.

In retrospect, I should have worked with her and been more open to other solutions for my issue — hiring the best-qualified candidates. Instead, I came at her like a bulldozer. I wasn't open to the possibility I might be wrong about changing the team's title. I wasn't open to there being a different reason why she was "protective" of the title and instead assumed it was a VP turf battle.

I successfully changed the titles, and we hired several talented content strategists to round out our team. But because of the way I approached this project, I got feedback from my manager that the way I'd handled it wasn't great, and it negatively affected my performance review.

I would have been more successful if I had been open and taken the time to understand what her motivations were and what issues were important to her. I could have found common ground rather than coming in and trying to prove my point.

I also could have asked for her help in solving the problem. In my experience, people respond better to a request for help than being told what to do. A request gives them the opportunity to say yes or no — they can at least consider the request before flat-out saying no.

Why did I feel the need to prove my point rather than approach this collaboratively? Because of my own FONBE. I feared being seen as someone who wouldn't advocate for her team. I was afraid that I wouldn't be able to hire the best people for the work we needed to do. I bought into stereotypes about being "tough" and "authoritative" as a leader. Yes, there is a time and place for those qualities, but a more collaborative approach would have benefitted me in this case.

Leadership guru Stephen Covey wrote the bestseller *The 7 Habits of Highly Effective People*. Habit 5, Seek to First

Understand, Then to Be Understood, is another way of bringing attention to openness. Covey encourages empathy in readers, advocating for listening first with the intent to understand before trying to make your point and prove that *you're* right. You have to be willing to be a better listener in order to be open.

In my coaching training with Co-Active Training Institute (CTI), I learned about the three listening levels. Level 1 is the listening we often tend to do, which is hearing what the other person is saying, but simultaneously thinking about how it relates to you. For example, your friend might be telling you about a trip she's planning to Italy, and as you hear her describe the places she wants to see, you're thinking about when you went to the local Italian restaurant and how you'd like to plan a trip to Italy. Or maybe, you've been to Italy, and you want to give her recommendations, and you're thinking about places you visited, and the next thing you know, she's looking at you funny because she asked a question, but you didn't catch it because your mind was enjoying some bruschetta and an Aperol spritz.

Level 2 is when you're able to focus more on what she's saying and really listen to what she's talking about. You might even ask some open-ended questions to encourage more sharing. "What are you looking forward to the most?" "What's your favorite Italian food?" etc. And when she answers, you get more curious. "Tell me more." You're completely focused on what your friend is saying. You are 100 percent there for her.

Level 3 is where it gets wider and deeper. Not only are you intently listening to what your friend is saying, but you're also listening to what's not being said. You are tuned in to her body language, the tone of her voice when she hesitates, and when she's excited, the energy in the room, what you sense from your friend, and what you're hearing.

Improving your listening skills by remembering to stay in Level 2 or 3 enables you to better understand someone else's point of view without missing out on what they're trying to tell you because you're listening to your own mind in Level 1.

You Need Strength to Be Open

When I was younger and less experienced, I confused "being open" with "taking time to listen to people share their opinion and then trying to convince them that I'm right." I was open to listening to their views, so that means I'm open, right? I scheduled the meeting with the VP, so I was "open" to feedback, yes? Nope. I'd made up my mind, and I would not be deterred.

The more I've interacted with people from different backgrounds and perspectives, the more I've learned that being open means being willing to be wrong and inviting differing opinions to pressure-test my views. Or at least being willing to loosen up my grip on my firmly held beliefs. As you've probably noticed, we humans don't like being wrong. We'd often rather be right than happy.

I didn't realize how much inner strength is required to be open — to admit to others, not just yourself, that you were wrong about something or misjudged someone. Openness requires an inner strength of knowing who *you* are and what is important to you — the aforementioned "Self-Awareness" from Chapter 2. Becoming more certain of who you are and what you want for your life allows you to be open to other perspectives because you're considering those perspectives from a solid foundation, not a shaky quicksand pit of self-doubt.

I've been fortunate to have opportunities that challenged my openness and helped me grow as a person. I was successful in my role as one of the first women to fly in a combat squadron because I had empathy for the men I flew with. I was open to viewing the world through their perspective. That doesn't mean I agreed with them, but I could mentally put myself in their shoes and imagine what this experience was like for them. They weren't used to having women around, which was a huge change for them, too.

Some were open to the change, others weren't, but they were forced to accept it. For those who were open, I was viewed as a fellow aviator, trained accordingly, and treated as a fellow squadron mate. For those who weren't open to the change, nothing I did was good enough, and they weren't willing to change their mind. Thankfully, the S-3B fleet squadron I served in was full of men in the former category. But many of my fellow female aviators were in squadrons with men who couldn't open their minds to the possibility that a woman could fly a jet as well (or better!) than they could. And unfortunately, those squadrons were worse off because of the inability of the leaders to get over their biases.

Be Open to Opportunities Beyond What You Think Are Possible or Probable

Every year, the graduate students at Wharton produce a major musical show called The Wharton Follies, which is performed several times in Philadelphia. We also performed in New York City because we have a lot of alumni there. Our cast and band spent a day in a studio in Philadelphia, recording the songs on a CD, which we sold to raise money to produce the show.

I loved writing and acting in the show my first year. I spent more time on Follies than on some of my business classes. At Wharton, we had a grading system that included a "QC" — a "Qualified Credit," which is like a D — you passed the class, but barely. Every student has a "bank" of six QCs you can earn and still get an MBA. I burned through a couple of my six allowable QCs in my first year because I loved working on the Follies so much. I wanted to be one of Wharton Follies' three directors for the second year. I thought I would get picked because of my enthusiasm and dedication to the show.

Typically, the way the outgoing three directors choose the incoming directors is to designate one person as the musical director, one as the acting director, and one as a choreographer. Two of my fellow cast members, who were incredibly musically talented, got picked for the musical director and acting director, no surprise there. The third spot was between me and another woman who had also done a lot of dancing. I'd thought I would get the choreographer-director position because I was a good dancer and had helped create some of the dances.

But the outgoing directors chose her instead of me. I was super disappointed because I loved doing it so much and already had a ton of ideas I wanted to do for the next year's show. Plus, let's be honest; it hurt my ego.

After the announcement, I was heartbroken. I took it personally, even though my classmate who had been chosen was a talented dancer and absolutely deserved to be in the role. My writer friends and the new directors came over and said, "We like writing with you. And if you want to be a head writer with us, we'd love to have you as a head writer."

I could have sulked and said, "No, thanks, I wanted to be a director, and I wasn't chosen for that, so forget it." But thankfully, I was open to other opportunities to help shape the show and contribute to the production's success.

I was grateful and delighted to have this opportunity for a leadership role in the Follies. As it turns out, as a head writer, I had a lot of control and authority over the show's content. Ironically, I wouldn't have been able to do that as a director.

Plus, the woman chosen to choreograph the show was super cool about it and asked me to choreograph one of the numbers.

The two other head writers and I worked together well. We balanced each other perfectly in our writing and sense of humor. The three of us and our talented writing team delivered a top-notch script that the directors and cast loved. It turned out to be one of my favorite writing experiences because we built upon one another's ideas and laughed all the time. And so, the second year, The Wharton Follies turned into one of my favorite experiences of my life because I had so much fun writing it and then performing it and working with the three directors. But if I hadn't been open to accepting a role that was different than what I thought I should have, I would have missed out on it.

Fear Is Your Friend

It's difficult to be open when you are afraid. Let's talk about that f-word: *fear*.

You might be surprised to hear this, but fear is not a horrible thing to be eradicated from your life. Don't buy into the "BE FEARLESS" hype. Fear is your friend... but probably not in the way you might expect.

First, let's think about what fear is. Back to the dictionary: Fear is an unpleasant emotion caused by the belief that someone or something is dangerous, likely to cause pain or a threat.

Ooh! Key word there: *belief*. Meaning it's in your head.

Yes, some fears are healthy and keep us from dying, or, as we used to like to say in the Navy, from "morting ourselves." Fear of standing on the edge of something tall, fear of eating things we know will poison us, fear of out-of-control animals that might bite us... do you see the trend? Fear of things that will kill us. *It's a biological protection mechanism.* The human body is amazing in that way. That innate desire to avoid that which is likely to kill us is one of two things that has kept the human species going. The other, of course, is the desire to mate, but we won't get into that here; this is not that kind of book.

So, you have physical reactions when you feel you are in situations that risk your life. Do you also notice those sensations when you are in uncomfortable situations that are not life-threatening, like speaking in public? Asking for something (a date with your crush, a promotion at work, etc.) where there's a likelihood you'll be rejected? Maybe you feel it in your stomach? Your spine? Your intestines? That physical sensation is there because your body is doing what it thinks it's supposed to do: keep you from harm.

We similarly rationalize away the things we want in our life because fear keeps us from moving forward. We've been conditioned to think of all the negative "what-ifs" to weigh whether a decision would benefit us. I engaged in that catastrophic thinking, as described in the previous chapter. But what if, instead of thinking about all the things that could go wrong, we thought about all the things that could go right? And what if we trusted that whatever happens is the right thing to happen?

I'm not saying I'm happy or cheery when bad things happen. But what I've found in my own life is that the more I've gotten in touch with what I want in my life, and then become open to possibilities for how that might show up in my life, the happier and more fulfilled I've become.

And when bad things happen, I let myself feel the emotion that comes up, but then I decide how long I want to keep feeling it. At some point, that emotion is not serving me well, and I need to choose to move forward. It sounds simple, but it is not easy. There is comfort in feeling that we're in control. Letting go of control and being open to possibilities is uncomfortable because we want to control the outcome, and we don't want to admit we're not as powerful as we'd like to be. Why do we want power and control? Because we're afraid we won't be able to live our lives as we want to. We don't have faith that things will work out.

Here are four ways to embrace your fear:

1. **Ask for support**. Talk with someone. Getting your fears out into the open is one of the best ways to manage them. In talking with others, you might learn strategies from friends who have been through similar struggles. And, of course, I recommend working with a coach! I love my friends, but they don't hold me (figuratively) like my coaches do. No bird (or person) soars on its own. Look at how birds fly in formation, in Vs, to optimize the lift of the flock. When you're struggling with fear, reach out to someone.

2. **Recognize your fear as an indicator of what matters to you**. If you're feeling fear and anxiety about something, it must be important enough to matter to you. Check in with yourself: Is this something that warrants your attention? If it doesn't really matter, then why be afraid of it?

3. **Consciously design your relationship with fear**. Imagine fear as an outside entity and have a conversation with it. What would you tell it? "Go away" is probably not going to be effective. You need to talk about it. Get curious. Maybe something like this: "Hey, fear. I see you've shown up again, and you're trying to steer my life. I know it's because you want to protect and keep me safe. I appreciate that you're looking out for me. I want you to know that we are going to be fine. I am confident I'm going to figure this out, so you don't have to

worry about me. We're going to be all right. Let's take a deep breath together, and then you can go hang out wherever it is that you hang out when you're not shaking me up."

4. **Move it!** Fear is a chemical reaction in our bodies. "Getting your heart rate up changes brain chemistry, increasing the availability of important anti-anxiety neurochemicals, including serotonin, gamma-aminobutyric acid (GABA), brain-derived neurotrophic factor (BDNF), and endocannabinoids," according to John J. Ratey, MD.[6] Walking in nature is one of my favorite ways to de-stress when I'm feeling anxious.

Change Is (Always) A'comin'

The only thing that doesn't change... is change. Our world and ourselves are always changing. Our bodies are literally changing every day. Most of your cells will be replaced by new cells every seven to 10 years. You're almost a completely new person! So why is it so difficult for us to be open to and even embrace change?

It gets back to comfort and self-protection. When we find something that works, we want to stick with it. And when we find something that doesn't work, we want to avoid it.

There's a famous story in the corporate training world about the four monkeys in a lab who are subjected to a spray of icy cold water every time one of them goes for a bunch of bananas hanging in the middle of their room. After a while, the monkeys learn not to reach for the bananas. The scientists replace one

---

6 John J. Ratey, MD, "Can exercise help treat anxiety?", October 24, 2019, Harvard Health Publishing, https://www.health.harvard.edu/blog/can-exercise-help-treat-anxiety-2019102418096.

of the original monkeys with a new monkey, and of course, he sees those yummy bananas and makes a beeline toward them but is beaten down by the three original monkeys who don't want to get sprayed again. The new monkey is thinking, wtf, but he doesn't want to get beaten up, so he stops reaching for the bananas. The scientists replace the other three original monkeys one by one, and the response repeats. New monkey sees bananas, reaches for them, gets beaten up, doesn't reach for bananas. The scientists even disconnect the icy water spray, but it doesn't matter because the monkeys have passed down this behavior. Once all the original monkeys have been replaced, the newer monkeys continue to smack down any monkey who enters the room and tries to go for the bananas because that's what they know.

In corporate training sessions, this story is brought out to help teams challenge processes and beliefs to sec if they're still true for them. Too often, when new employees ask, "Why are we doing X?" they are told, "Because we've always done it that way."

Outside of the corporate world, how many other examples are there of "We've always done it this way, so that's why we're doing it this way." We make assumptions without being open to other ways of living and interacting with others. Visionaries are able to look at how we do things and consider, "What if we did it a different way? Would that be better? How would it be better?"

The past is the past. We can't relive it; we can't change it. So, when I find myself longing for something that happened in the past, I try to catch myself and understand what the longing is about. Is it something I can bring into my life now? For example, if I recall fond memories from high school in the 1980s and I long for a simpler time (with the best music ever!), how could I bring more simplicity into my life? I mean, no one is stopping me from disconnecting from the internet and social media. If I really wanted to relive the 80s, I could shut down my accounts and limit myself to four TV stations and the local library to get my news and information.

Can I also recognize the not-so-great parts of that which I have probably overlooked in my attempt to romanticize the past? And can I ask myself, what is the benefit of spending this mental energy contemplating something that isn't reality anymore? When I was living it, it was my reality, but now it's a memory — fallible and easily contorted to embellish the good parts and minimize the bad.

This is why I scratch my head when I hear complaining about today's world and clinging to the idea of "the good ol' days." Instead of wishing for something that is impossible to recreate, why not decide what kind of world we want and start working together to effect changes to make *that* happen? I think it gets back to fear and the assumption that someone is going to have to lose if someone else is winning, and no one wants to be the loser.

Open Equals Growth Mindset

After Super Bowl LVII, the Philadelphia Eagles' quarterback, Jalen Hurts, shared his disappointment at his team's loss but shared this wisdom: "You either win, or you learn." I love that perspective. Rather than beat ourselves up by what we didn't accomplish (which we can't change because it's in the past), why not focus on what could be better next time?

One of the aspects of working in the technology industry that I enjoyed the most was the emphasis on "failing" fast. Try things, see what works and what doesn't. We were constantly looking for ways to improve products and services. There was no resting on laurels or getting complacent about what we offered. It reminded me of flying in the Navy — as a pilot; I was constantly scanning the instruments in the cockpit and looking outside the aircraft to ensure I was aviating and navigating well.

Remember, think of *"FAIL"* as an acronym: First Attempt in Learning. Failure has gotten a bad rap. We often learn more from our failures than from our successes.

I wonder if parents at the turn of the century were complaining about change and arguing with their teenagers, too. I can imagine the scene around a very fancy Victorian dining room table, with the patriarch opining, "What does that idiot Henry Ford think he's doing? I love our horses!" and the kids thinking, "I can't wait to get my hands on one of those Model Ts!"

Change can feel scary because it's uncertain. But really, besides death and taxes, what is guaranteed in life? Who, besides a group of scientists, could have predicted our world would experience a multi-year pandemic? Were we expecting that? No, but we dealt with it. We had to be open to changing our routines and the way we interacted in order to help contain and minimize coronavirus exposure. And we figured it out.

No one can predict everything about the future. And since we can't control the future, why not be open to possibility and loosen our tight grip around our firmly held beliefs about how our futures should be?

I'm a certified Positive Intelligence[7] coach. We support people with building their mental fitness, which we define as our capacity to respond to life's challenges with a positive rather than negative mindset. One aspect of this framework that I find intriguing is being open to the "other side" being 10 percent right. Wait, what? How can I have an opinion or perspective that

---

7 Positive Intelligence coaching is based on Shirzad Chamine's *New York Times* and *Wall Street Journal* bestseller *Positive Intelligence: Why Only 20% of Teams and Individuals Achieve Their True Potential and How You Can Achieve Yours* (Austin, TX: Greenleaf Book Group Press, 2012).

I firmly believe in, yet engage in a conversation with someone who disagrees with me with the assumption from the beginning that 10 percent of what I'm thinking is wrong and they're 10 percent right?

It doesn't mean we have to change our minds, but if you have strong self-awareness, you're more comfortable with challenging your beliefs. If we're not open to the possibility that we're not 100 percent correct in our views, we lose out on the opportunity to learn more about ourselves and others.

One of my favorite compliments, both to give and receive, is, "I never thought about it that way." I love reading books that open me up to new ways of looking at life and I've included many of them at the end in Resources.

One that recently rocked my world is *The Surrender Experiment* by Michael Singer. He describes his journey of an unplanned life, only responding to opportunities that crossed his path. For me, as a planner (#virgo, remember?) this blew my mind. How could anyone be that spontaneous? Reading about his success, and more importantly, his happiness and fulfillment, nudged me to start loosening my grip on future plans and be more open to opportunities.

I've had to reconcile this spontaneity with my belief that our intentions create our world. For example, I love creating vision boards because it reminds me of the things and experiences I want in my life. But creating a vision board is creating a vision, not a project plan or Gantt chart for how these things will come about in my life. A vision board is not dictating to the Universe exactly how I want my desires to show up. After reading *The Surrender Experiment*, I still believe we should have intentions about what we want to do in the world and how we want to be in it, in alignment with our values. But I am much more open now to accepting that those things and experiences will come into my life at the right time, not necessarily at the time I want them to.

I feel like change is challenging for us because uncertainty is uncomfortable. We want to know what is going to happen to us because being in control is comforting. But if you get comfortable with the fact that things are always changing, then you can become more adaptable. The importance of knowing your strengths and your values is that it gives you a solid foundation that can weather change. Self-awareness provides the strength to be open. Being open allows you to jiujitsu your way through the changes life throws at you, so instead of being knocked over, you absorb the energy and become even stronger.

You can go from the lowest low to the highest high. Even if you think all is lost, there's always hope. It's going to work out — maybe not as you think it should, but it's going to work out. I love the line from the movie *The Best Exotic Marigold Hotel*: "Everything will be all right in the end, so if it is not all right, it is not the end."

Be open to different possibilities.

Your Flight Plan

1. Get curious! Openness is a sense of curiosity about the world. Is there a topic you've wanted to learn about or an issue for which you'd like to be more informed? Set aside a few minutes each day for a week to do some internet sleuthing or read a book about it. Maybe there's a new skill you want to learn or a hobby you've always been interested in. Why wait? If you don't have local businesses that offer what you're interested in, YouTube is a cornucopia of "how-to" content for almost anything you've thought about learning.

2. Next time you find yourself in a disagreement with someone, rather than spending your energy trying to convince the other person that you're right, become incredibly curious about that person's position. Ask them questions as if you were interviewing someone for a documentary. Table your opinion and judgment and open up to what they have to say. You might surprise yourself that there's overlap on things you agree upon. That's a much better place to launch a negotiation.

3. What's something you're afraid of? Have a discussion about this fear. Journal your thoughts so you can reflect back on the conversation if that fear arises again.

4. Let's get literal — soar! Check out your local general aviation airports for a sample "discovery" flight. Being able to slip the surly bonds of gravity by flying around your neighborhood can reboot your routine by enabling you to see your world from a different angle, literally. If taking a flight is out of the question, find a playground and use the swings to get some lift into your life. Enjoy that feeling of weightlessness at the top of the arc. If it's a big swing, you might even get a little altitude to help shift your perspective.

"Faith is taking the first step even when you don't see the whole staircase."

—THE REVEREND DR. MARTIN LUTHER KING JR.

Chapter 4

APPRECIATION

"Be thankful for what you have; you'll end up having more. If you concentrate on what you don't have, you will never, ever have enough."

— OPRAH WINFREY

One of our main missions when I was flying the S-3B Viking onboard a carrier was inflight refueling. Vikings carried a "buddy store": a large tank of gas attached underneath our port (left) wing. During the recoveries (landings at the aircraft carrier), we'd fly in a left-hand pattern above the ship. If another jet was low on gas before entering the landing pattern, it would fly up and rendezvous with us. We'd extend the refueling basket, and they would use the refueling plug on their jets to plug into

S-3B Viking refueling an F/A-18 Hornet" Photo Credit: U.S. Navy photo by Cmdr. Thomas Lalor

the basket and receive enough gas so they could go around the landing pattern a few times.

Flying around in left-hand circles above the ship could feel routine... because we were just flying around in a left-hand circle and the other jets would come to us — the Chevron station in the sky. However, we did have one refueling mission that added some excitement to our flights — "hawking" a jet low on gas that was coming in to land on the carrier. As a pilot, I had to maneuver our jet to ensure that we were ahead of a landing jet in case they boltered or were waved off. The goal was for the pilot who was low on gas to be able to look up as they lifted off the flight deck and see me, the big ol' bag of gas in the sky right in front of them. Come to Mama!

Hawking involved some skillful maneuvering and flying formation off the jet in need. It was not nearly as thrilling and challenging as aerial combat maneuvering (aka dogfighting), but it was definitely more fun than turning left-hand circles in the sky.

One dark night (why is it always on the "dark and stormy" nights that stuff happens?), I hawked a F/A-18 pilot who was very low on gas. If he didn't get fuel from us, he wasn't going to be able to make it around one more time to try landing again. With the help of my navigator, we timed our hawk, so we arrived at the pilot's 11 o'clock position, and sure enough, the poor guy was waved off. Wave-offs happen when the pilot has not flown the plane within the acceptable parameters to ensure a safe landing, but sometimes, and in this case, pilots are waved off because the landing area is "fouled," meaning someone or something is within the landing area, making it unsafe for everyone.

After being waved off, he flew up, extended his refueling probe and took on a few thousand pounds of gas, then turned back and was able to land on the next attempt.

Afterward, he sought me out in the passageway and said, "Hey, Rowdy[8], thanks a bunch for the gas. You saved my life." Wow. I still get choked up when I think about this. I wasn't expecting a thank you for doing my job, a job I did every single day, but hearing him say that...well, I still remember it and his name to this day, almost 30 years later. Anytime, Chuck Billy!

The gratitude he shared made a lifelong impact on me, despite the fact that I was doing what I was expected to do.

As a leader in Silicon Valley companies, I felt disappointed when my fellow people managers dismissed the notion of saying thank you to people for doing their job. "Well, it's their job, it's what they're supposed to be doing," they'd say. "Why should I praise them for meeting the minimum?"

I would respond with the saying from Confucius, "Praise is like sand in an oyster: a little causes a pearl, but too much spoils it."

I think there's a difference between acknowledgment and praise. Everyone wants to feel like what they're doing matters, otherwise, why be there? Can't we acknowledge the effort? Praise is deserved for a job well done, but I also feel like it's important to show appreciation for showing up and being part of a team.

When I worked at Google, we had an annual employee survey nicknamed "Googlegeist," which measured many indicators of employee satisfaction. One of the findings was that the happiest Googlers were the ones who felt the most grateful for the perks they received. And BTW, they were some amazing on-site perks:

---

8 My callsign (the nicknames aviators use instead of our real names) was Rowdy because it rhymes with my last name, Draude. You don't get to choose your callsign, you usually have it bestowed upon you by your squadron mates, typically because of something stupid you've been caught doing, but often it's a word that rhymes with or plays off of your last name.

subsidized massages, free gourmet food for three meals a day, and nap pods. Being able to appreciate the good things in our lives correlates to happiness.

What happens during those moments in your life when you feel wonderful and when things are going your way, even if just for a moment? Like when another driver lets you merge on a crowded highway, or you find those extra fries in the bottom of the In-n-Out Burger bag? Do you feel appreciation in those moments? Do you actually say thank you? Appreciating the small wins in life can help you feel more gratitude on a larger scale when times are challenging.

Appreciation and Gratitude

I use the terms *appreciation* and *gratitude* interchangeably here because I feel they are so similar, and also because SOAR works and SOGR doesn't really make sense. Work with me here, okay?

What exactly is *gratitude*? According to the Harvard Medical School:

> "Gratitude is a thankful appreciation for what an individual receives, whether tangible or intangible. With gratitude, people acknowledge the goodness in their lives. In the process, people usually recognize that the source of that goodness lies at least partially outside themselves. As a result, gratitude also helps people connect to something larger than themselves as individuals — whether to other people, nature, or a higher power."[9]

9 "Giving Thanks Can Make You Happier," Harvard Health Publishing, Harvard Medical School https://www.health.harvard.edu/healthbeat/giving-thanks-can-make-you-happier.

I hope that after reading the previous chapter you are open to the possibility that cultivating more gratitude in your life will help you to soar and that I don't have to beat you over the head with research and statistics to "prove" that gratitude has a positive effect on your life.

However, a cursory search on the internet or a prompt on ChatGPT surfaces multiple studies supporting the positive effect of gratitude:

1. Expressing gratitude regularly can increase happiness levels by about 25 percent. (Source: Emmons & McCullough, *Journal of Personality and Social Psychology*, 2003)

2. Grateful people report fewer symptoms of illness and are more likely to engage in healthy behaviors. (Source: Wood, Froh, & Geraghty, 2010)

3. Keeping a gratitude journal for as little as three weeks can result in better sleep and increased energy levels. (Source: Emmons & McCullough, 2003)

4. Grateful individuals have been found to have lower levels of depression and anxiety. (Source: Wood, Froh, & Geraghty, 2010) … and so on and so on.

It's a biological need for humans to feel connected. From our prehistoric days of gathering around a fire to stay warm, we need to feel like we belong. Not belonging meant death — literally. These days, rejection feels like metaphorical death because it taps into that physiological need to belong and connect.

This is why appreciation is important. Gestures and words relay the information we need in order to know that we do belong and that we're not going to get kicked out of that metaphorical Neanderthal cave.

My favorite band in the world is Crowded House. I've been a fan since the '80s. Whenever they tour, I treat myself to the best seat in the house I can get. During their last North American tour, I was fortunate enough to catch three of their concerts, and for the final one I attended, I bought a ticket in the center of the third row.

When Neil, Nick, Mitchell, Elroy, and Liam walked onstage and launched into their opening song, "World Where You Live," I felt so much joy to be in the same space as my favorite band surrounded by people who share my love for their music. It occurred to me that their music has brought me joy for most of my adult life. I felt a huge sense of appreciation for that moment in time at the concert. It rose like warmth in my chest to a glow on my smiling face. My feet were on the ground, but my soul was soaring.

This intense sense of gratitude has stayed with me ever since. When I go to sleep, I try to recall that feeling, either by reliving that joyous moment in my mind or by reflecting on something else from the day I'm grateful for or thinking about my love for my children. I find I sleep better if my mind is focused on something I appreciate, rather than racing around, thinking about the future, or regretting something from the past.

Do you experience the 3:30 a.m. wakeups? Before I went through my coaching training, this was a regular occurrence for me. It started around the time I got divorced, which was also the time I was serving as the COO of a startup and my kids were in grade school. I had a lot on my mind, and I was constantly trying to plan for every possibility. When I started cultivating a greater sense of appreciation for the good things in my life and began letting go of controlling everything I could in my world, I began to experience more inner peace.

Have you heard of the saying "Let go and let God?" I'm not a religious person, despite being brought up in the Catholic faith.

I'm glad that many people — including my parents, brothers, and friends — find comfort and strength in their faith.

I have a different kind of faith. I don't view "God" as a gendered entity that is external to us. I view "God" as a universal energy that is within all of us as we live on this planet. When I think of "Let go and let God," I'm reminded of my belief that there is a divine plan for us, whether you want to refer to it as God, Allah, Yaweh, the Universe, or however your path of faith refers to its higher power. The struggle and unhappiness occur for me when I refuse to let go of my expectations and preconceived notions of what my life should be like. When I became more in touch with what really mattered to me (not to my parents or my partner or what society has historically defined as "success") and opened myself to the possibility that there might be better options for living the life I want, I was amazed by how doors began opening for me to live that life.

I again need to emphasize that it's not like I've been sitting on the sofa, eating TimTams (chocolate wafer cookies from Australia that are absolutely scrumptious) and waiting for the Universe to deliver the things I want into my lap. I'm setting the intentions and I'm doing the work. I'm also fortunate to be in a privileged position in the world, where some things have been easier for me than for others from historically marginalized communities.

What does this have to do with appreciation? I go back to the quote from Oprah at the beginning of this chapter: "Be thankful for what you have; you'll end up having more." When I had those 3:30 a.m. wakeups, by feeling appreciation for the good things in my life and minimizing my thinking about what I felt was lacking, somehow my brain quieted down and stopped waking me up in the middle of the night to solve the inadequacies in my life. By focusing on gratitude, I believe my brain trained itself to trust that there would be more things to be grateful for and, therefore, it could take a break and get some sleep. I'm not a scientist and this could be complete baloney, but it works for me.

One of my favorite simple ways to tap into gratitude is when I wash my hands. I engage almost all of my senses in this short meditative experience. I feel the temperature of the water and the suds of the soap, I smell the scent of the soap fragrance, I see the bubbles and the water flowing from the faucet, and I hear the water rinsing my hands. If it's a lemon-scented soap, I might imagine tasting a lemon (but don't taste the soap!).

I think of how grateful I am for indoor plumbing and for a nice-smelling soap, and for warm water. Maybe I'm grateful for having that moment of taking a really short break in a very busy day. When I was experiencing super-busy days at work, I joked with my coworkers about the UTI (urinary tract infection) days because I barely had time to go to the bathroom. Just a few seconds of focus and appreciation builds a muscle of noticing and appreciating the good things in our lives. It might only last for two seconds, but two seconds is better than zero, and over time, this builds into a perspective of appreciation.

My dad shared with me a story of dining at a restaurant with my mother a couple of years ago. Their waitress had done a great job of serving them, despite being incredibly busy and managing several tables by herself. When she brought the check to the table, my dad asked if he could speak with her manager. Her face fell, and she asked, "I'm so sorry, is there something wrong?" My dad said, "Oh, no, not at all, in fact, quite the opposite. I wanted to tell your manager what a great job you're doing." The waitress burst into tears. My parents were shocked. The waitress said, "No one has ever done anything like that." She wiped away her tears and proudly brought her manager over to the table to receive my parents' gratitude.

We often find the time to complain when we feel we haven't received good service, but how often do we make sure to acknowledge and appreciate people who are going above and beyond? A simple gesture of gratitude can make a huge difference in someone's life.

I have a friend who carries around $10 Starbucks gift cards with him and gives them out randomly to firefighters, emergency medical technicians, and law enforcement officers as a token of appreciation for their service to their communities. I admire his generosity and thoughtfulness.

* * *

I'd like to share the concept of emotional frequencies. Have you noticed the "vibe" in a room? You may have walked into a group bursting with joyous energy, or conversely, a conference room filled with people where the environment felt heavy and oppressive. Gratitude is around "joy" level. Bringing more gratitude into our lives can help move us up the emotional vibration chart.

Why am I sharing this chart? Is it for real; do emotions have "vibrations"? I don't know, but I find the concept helpful. Here's how to use the chart:

When you are feeling a negative emotion, find it on the chart. For example, let's say someone cut you off in traffic and you're feeling angry. Find "Anger" on the chart and notice which emotions are higher up. What's a way you can shift out of your anger to an emotion that's higher up? Can you move from "anger" to "pride"? Maybe you realize that you really love your car, and it angered you that some yahoo driving while looking at their phone might damage it? Or could you move up to courage? You're handling a multi-ton moving vehicle. It takes

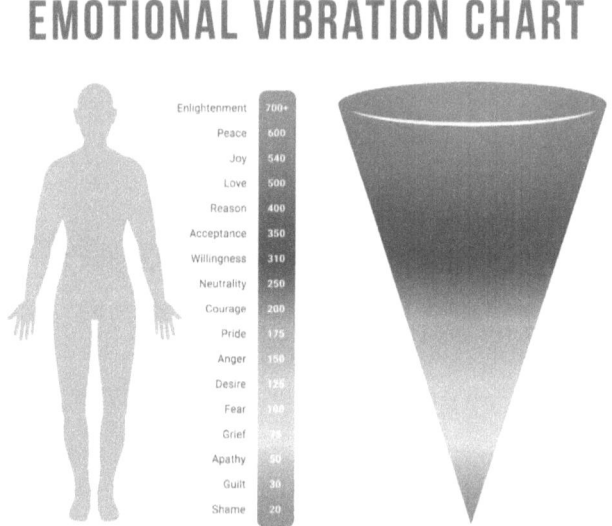

THE HUMAN
EMOTIONAL VIBRATION CHART

Enlightenment	700+
Peace	600
Joy	540
Love	500
Reason	400
Acceptance	350
Willingness	310
Neutrality	250
Courage	200
Pride	175
Anger	150
Desire	125
Fear	100
Grief	75
Apathy	50
Guilt	30
Shame	20

Image used with permission from @ wisnukrist via depositphotos.com

inner strength and confidence to do that! Feel the courage you have to be out on the road with these rotten drivers!

BTW, do you see that it's not expected for you to automatically jump up to acceptance, reason, or love? I wouldn't expect myself to jump immediately from saying, "Get your slow butt out of the passing lane, jack ass" to "Hey, beautiful fellow human being, thanks for the reminder to slow down and appreciate this drive." But maybe eventually, you might refrain from anger in traffic and instead find empathy for other drivers. That man might be late for his job through no fault of his own and worried he won't be able to feed his family. That woman might have just received horrible news and is having a hard time focusing on the road. Or maybe they truly are being jerks. I don't know, but I personally would rather let a jerk cut in front of me than get pissed off at someone who just received traumatic news and carry that anger around with me all day.

Also, I don't want you to think I drive around with a smile on my face, letting everyone merge 100 feet before the lanes come together and smiling at drivers who dangerously cut me off. Driving is my practice ground for working on living at a higher vibration. My typical first response when another driver doesn't signal a turn or speeds down the right lane of the freeway or disregards one of many other road rules is to proclaim them an f-ing idiot. But over time, I've managed to be less reactive and move up that chart a little faster than before.

If you're not sure which emotion you're feeling, this handy wheel[10] helps to identify some core emotions, both positive and negative. The first step toward moving from negative to positive emotions is noticing that you're feeling an emotion, and this chart is handy for identifying what truly ails you. You can't soar if you're weighed down by anger, fear, sadness, disappointment, or general bad feelings.

Start in the center of the circle and move out until you narrow down the emotion you're feeling, then reflect on what's coming up for you. Perhaps journal about what you're feeling or, even better, talk it out with a good friend who can help you explore the stories going through your head and support you on determining if they're actually true or if it's only negative emotions clouding your vision.

10 Willcox, G. (1982). The Feeling Wheel: A Tool for Expanding Awareness of Emotions and Increasing Spontaneity and Intimacy. Transactional Analysis Journal, 12(4), 274–276. https://doi.org/10.1177/036215378201200411

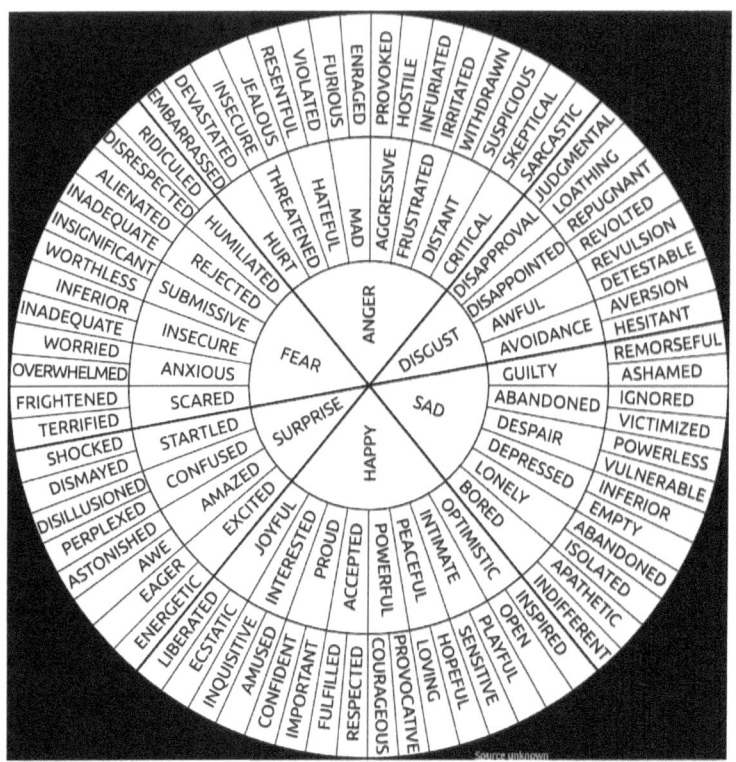

Source unknown

Your Flight Plan:

1. Set an alarm or put a Post-it Note by your bed, and before you go to sleep tonight, think about your day and write down three things you appreciated about it. Even better, start a "gratitude journal." When researchers Robert A. Emmons and Michael E. McCullough conducted a study asking participants to record five things they were grateful for once a month, writing only one sentence per topic, they saw improvements after only two months. According to a *NY Times* article[11], "the

---

11 https://www.nytimes.com/2011/11/22/science/a-serving-of-gratitude-brings-healthy-dividends.html

people keeping the gratitude journal were more optimistic and felt happier. They reported fewer physical problems and spent more time working out." Consider making this a habit. Going to sleep in a state of gratitude might help you feel more at peace, rather than rehashing the conflicts of the day. Aim for writing down five different things every day that you're grateful for.

2. As you go to sleep, think about a time in your life when you experienced extreme joy and focus on what it *felt* like. Don't just think about it, really feel it again. Feel that warmth and energy in your chest, in your heart. Maybe it brings a smile to your face and a tear to your eye.

3. Model a culture of appreciation in your life by sincerely thanking people for the work they're doing or kind gestures, like holding a door open.

4. It's not enough to feel appreciation. You need to tell others you are grateful for them. Try this exercise with a partner or friend: Share with them what you appreciate about them, and then share what you appreciate about yourself. Then they do the same.

5. Go bigger with shared appreciation: Write a short letter (300-500 words) to someone who has had a positive influence on your life. Rather than mail it, share it with them in person and leave the letter as a souvenir so they can bask in the appreciation you shared. Soaring is better together!

6. Reach out to someone you haven't talked with in a long time and reconnect. Let them know you're thinking about them. Everyone needs to know they matter, and sometimes in our busy existence, we forget the impact that we have on others.

Human beings need other human beings to survive. We are a communal species.

7. Do something for yourself each day. Sounds simple, but we often find excuses for why we can't. We *choose* not to. What are your priorities? Is personal fulfillment one of them, or are you still convincing yourself that you don't matter enough to prioritize your own needs?

I recommend choosing joy. Take out a piece of paper (or open your laptop if you're inclined to be digital) and make a list of at least 10 activities and things that bring you joy, then commit to doing it once a day.

Here are some of the things from my list:
- Eat a small piece of chocolate.
- Take a short walk and engage my senses: Look at the scenery, hear the noises, smell the air.
- Smell something amazing, like flowers or a freshly cut lemon or my daughter's hair (tougher to do now that she's 19 and thinks this is weird).
- Read a chapter from a favorite book.
- Moisturize my hands.
- Stretch.
- Take a 15-minute nap in a sunny spot on the sofa.
- Pet my cats and enjoy how much they appreciate the gesture.
- Draw for 10 minutes.
- Lie on my back outside and watch clouds float by.
- Work on a coloring book page.
- Watch a funny video on YouTube or an '80s music video. I recommend comedy rather than drama because you want to feel joy.

- Put on a favorite tune and have a short solo dance party. No one is watching. And if they are, who cares? Maybe they'll join in and experience joy alongside you.

8. Get a pack of Post-it Notes. Write "SOAR" in clear, large letters, and place one wherever there is a sink in your home. The next time you wash your hands, look at that note and bring your attention to that moment. Feel the temperature of the water on your hands. Smell the scent of the soap you're using. Listen to the water flowing from the faucet and splashing through your fingers. Look at the bubbles that form and wash away. Feel appreciation for these 15 to 20 seconds of sensory immersion.

"As we express our gratitude, we must never forget that the highest appreciation is not to utter words, but to live by them."

— JOHN F. KENNEDY

Chapter 5

RESPONSIBILITY

"Most people do not really want freedom because freedom involves responsibility, and most people are frightened of responsibility."

—SIGMUND FREUD

Several years ago, I worked at a small fintech startup that enabled remote payments with cash. I was sitting on the couch at home watching something on TiVo (okay, maybe it was more than several years!). And like any startup employee, of course, I checked email constantly, 24/7.

A few minutes after 10 p.m. I started seeing horrifying emails in our company inbox.

Things like:
You should burn in hell.
Who do you think you are?
You are the worst possible company ever.
I hope you're proud of yourselves.

What's going on? This is weird, I thought as I literally scratched my head, trying to figure out what was up.
I looked at the website and didn't see anything odd. Then another email came in, and it referenced *The Colbert Report*.
Huh, I thought.

Fortunately, this was back when TiVos recorded the East Coast version of *The Colbert Report* (I lived in California at the time). I started watching it, and, lo and behold, there was our company's logo next to Stephen Colbert's face. I guess the show's writers had seen our press coverage the month prior in the *New York Times* and thought our company was ripe for roasting, presenting us as a company that offers online credit to kids.

Colbert skewered the company. It was a funny piece. Stephen Colbert is hilarious, but it misrepresented our business.

I could not believe that our company was on *The Colbert Report*. We had no idea they were going to talk about us.

I went into an emergency mishap mode. It was like being back in the Navy. Every squadron duty desk has a mishap folder with a step-by-step checklist of what to do if there is an accident.

I had the opportunity to put a mishap plan into action one night when I was standing duty in 1998 at the S-3B Fleet Replacement Squadron, VS-41, at NAS North Island in San Diego. I earlier shared the story of reporting to VS-41 to learn how to fly the S-3B Viking; now I was one of the instructor pilots. We were training a batch of aviators on how to land the Viking on an aircraft carrier, and that evening several instructors were flying with student Viking pilots out at San Clemente Island. San Clemente is a fantastic place to practice nighttime carrier landings because it's far enough away from the West Coast to get good and dark, so you get a better sensation of what it's like to land on a carrier at night.

As an instructor, we had to stand duty every few weeks or so. It was usually pretty chill, mostly listening to the other instructors exchanging stories about going to the airlines after getting out of the Navy and which carrier was best — United, Delta or American. I wasn't planning on going to the airlines after I finished my service, but I enjoyed listening to the usual aviator bullshit and jokes being cracked at one another's expense. My laughter was interrupted by the phone ringing — a landline.

I picked it up and casually answered, "VS-41 Ready Room, how can I help you?"

The voice on the other end was Lt. Walt "Sarge" Slaughter. He knew I was on duty since he had two hours earlier briefed all of the aviators in the Ready Room before flying out to San Clemente to land and start his duty as the head landing signal officer, grading all of the aviators on how well they performed their field carrier landing practice.

"Rowdy, we have a jet down. Two good chutes," he said matter-of-factly.

This caught my attention.

"Are you shitting me?" I blurted. Sarge was famous for his practical jokes, including one of my favorites, "Lights on deck!" referring to the call LSOs make to inexperienced pilots who land on the carrier at night and forget to turn off their exterior lights, a big no-no because it reduces everyone's night vision and therefore makes the flight deck even more dangerous. Sarge's "Lights on deck" was a bar trick that consisted of surreptitiously sticking a full open matchbook into an unsuspecting aviator's back jean pocket and then lighting the matches on fire, yelling, "LIGHTS ON DECK!" We'd all laugh at the joke's victim swatting at his own ass to put out the fire.

But this was no joke.

"Negative, start the mishap plan," he replied.

"Roger that," I said quickly, hanging up the phone with one hand while reaching for the mishap plan with the other.

Thankfully, both aviators involved in the mishap suffered only minor injuries and were flying again a few weeks after. The jet they were flying unfortunately did not fare as well after crashing onto the island. It was completely destroyed.

Our startup was less than a year old with about 10 employees. We had no mishap plan or plan for crisis communications. So, I fell back on my Navy training: Aviate, Navigate, Communicate.

AVIATE: The Navy version — Is the plane flying? If the plane is in any danger of not staying in the air, then don't worry about navigating or talking to that air traffic controller who's sitting on the ground with a cup of coffee and a Twinkie (no disrespect to ATCs, they deserve all the caffeine and sugar for the tough job they have!). Make sure you are not about to crash your plane.

The civilian version — Is anyone in the company in immediate danger?

Answer: Being misrepresented on *The Colbert Report* might feel horrible and the emails weren't fun to read but no one was about to die, so short answer: No.

NAVIGATE: The Navy version — Am I flying the plane to where it needs to go and therefore not wasting gas? Am I going to where I'm expected to go?

The civilian version — What's the next step to take?

Answer: Time to call the CEO.

I called the CEO right away and let him know, even though he was out to dinner, celebrating his birthday. I explained the situation — *The Colbert Report*, the number of emails we were getting, the sudden spike in traffic to our website. We discussed our strategy, and I started executing it while he finished his cake and enjoyed the last few minutes of his birthday before we dealt with the shitstorm.

COMMUNICATE: The Navy version: Only after you've ensured you and your crew and the jet are safe and executing your mission, then start talking with people outside the aircraft. Who needs to know what you're doing?

The civilian version — What communications need to go out to deal with this crisis?

Answer: Inform investors, employees, and customers. Let others know what you're doing so they're informed and not surprised. Also, they can help you.

I wrote an email for the CEO to send to our investors to let them know what was going on.

Then we hatched a plan for the CEO to write a response that we would post on the website, so when people came to see who this horrible company was, they would see our story. We also reached out to *The Colbert Report* and asked them to correct the error. (They didn't).

We knew we had truth on our side. We knew what the company was about. We were not doing what they said we were doing. But it made us realize we were representing ourselves in a way that could be misinterpreted. For example, the website had a cartoon character of a duck, so people might have thought it was for kids. The CEO was very attached to this character and thought it was fun.

We learned from the experience. We took responsibility for our part in a misunderstanding and misrepresentation of what our business was about.

We did a duck-ectomy and took the mascot off the site. We made it more professional. We got through it.

The funny thing is that the saying "There's no such thing as bad PR" is true. We got a lot of hate email but we also received a bunch of business inquiries.

When people realized what our business actually was, a lot of companies wanted to work with us because the payment system was compelling. What began as a crisis turned into a huge opportunity for our little startup.

Although this story had a happy ending, I couldn't watch *The Colbert Report* for a few months after that event. Eventually, Colbert skewered another company, and I thought it was funny. It's funny when it's not your own company.

Looking back on the situation, we realized we had a good plan, we executed it well, we contained the damage and even came out stronger than before. We took responsibility for some poor prior decisions, and we learned from them.

* * *

If you want to SOAR and live the life of your dreams, you have to take 100 percent responsibility for your life. All too often, in today's world, responsibility is equated with a burden: the "weight" of responsibility. However, when we take true responsibility, it is the path of freedom. Freedom comes from responsibility.

This can be confronting for people, especially those who look at life as something that is happening TO them, rather than FOR them. It's normal to be put off by this statement. Have you ever heard people say, "I didn't ask for this." Have you said it? I have! Well, no shit, no one asks for the crappy things that happen in their lives. As the saying goes, shit happens. How we respond to the shit is how we design our lives. The thoughts we decide to have are how we design our lives.

Taking responsibility for our lives means reflecting on those crappy situations and considering how we contributed to them. Let me be clear here: This is not about victim-shaming. People are wronged every day through no fault of their own. I'm talking about how our words and actions contribute to the world and how we show up in it.

For example, if you love to judge others and gossip about people because it makes you feel better about yourself, but then you complain about how horrible the world is, you might want to reflect on how you're contributing to that negative energy in the world.

Victor Frankl, the Jewish-Austrian psychiatrist who survived a WWII concentration camp, wrote a must-read book called *Man's Search for Meaning*. One of my favorite quotes from his book is: "Between stimulus and response, there is a space. In that space is our power to choose our response. In our response lies our growth and our freedom."

Frankl realized while clinging to life in a Nazi concentration camp, that his captors could not strip away this power. His "response-ability" was the one freedom that could not be taken away.

Being responsible means giving up all your excuses, all your victim stories, all the reasons why you can't and why you haven't up until now, and all your blaming of outside circumstances. Simple, but not easy. You have to give them all up forever.

This is hard to hear. "Wait, if someone is being a jerk to me, I'm supposed to figure out how I have a part in that?" Yes, you are. It's difficult sometimes. But every relationship we have — whether with a loved one, a coworker, a stranger on the street — we all have a responsibility in how we show up. We're not responsible for the other person's reactions. I'm talking about our personal choice in how *we* respond.

Responsibility and Response-ability

The Frankl quote reminds us that we do have the choice about how we respond. Many of us are used to reacting — an automatic response that we are conditioned to have because we didn't learn to regulate our emotions. And because, let's be honest, there's short-term satisfaction in reactions. Telling someone off feels good: We're releasing our emotions, we're being heard, we're feeling some justice. Reacting feels good in the moment, but there's that little voice inside of us thinking... mmm, maybe that should have stayed in my brain instead of going through my mouth. Instead of thinking of the long game and how to best construct communication that serves our long-term goals or the relationship, we want the short-term fix.

Response-ability is really creativity, and we are all creative beings. We can choose how we want to respond. Again, simple but not easy. We are responsible for the emotional field that we are creating through our facial expressions, the tone of our voice, eye contact or lack thereof. We are impacting others all the time, and often not in the way we intended.

Being Responsible for Your Life

There are two types of conversations you have that design your life: the ones in your head and the ones you have with other people.

You read about the ones in your head in Chapter 2. They're often driven by fear, so once you learn to recognize that and start embracing the fear, you can be in a relationship with it and manage it better. Remember the exercise to have a conversation with your fears? Putting thoughts into words on a page gives them life and the opportunity to be fully considered, examined, and processed.

The next step is to have conversations with other people. Have you seen videos of ants communicating with one another? One ant runs up to another, and they rub their antennae together, sharing pheromones that transmit information. Then they go run around and find a couple of other ants and rub antennae, and so on. The information they transmit is carried and transferred from one ant to the next, around a colony of thousands.

I think of the conversations we have with other people as an extremely slowed-down version of ant interactions. Let's say I have a conversation with Bob at work. We talk about projects, and we exchange information. After the meeting, I stop by the restroom (must not be a UTI day!) and then run into Sue in the hallway. She asks me about a different project, and I give her a 30-second update. Both Bob and Sue have received information from me and are carrying it around in their brains, and I've picked up information from them and am adding it to what I'm thinking about. The content and emotion that's shared is shaping our lives.

Disagreement is unavoidable. This would be a boring world if we agreed on everything. But we should be responsible for creating safe environments where discourse can occur, and disagreements can be resolved peacefully. It's easier to shut out people who don't agree with you, but it also denies you the opportunity for personal growth and maybe even opening up someone else's mind by showing up as a curious, non-judgmental human being.

"Everybody wants to save the earth; nobody wants to help Mom do the dishes."

—PJ O'ROURKE

I like this quote because it reminds us that we can exercise responsibility in small ways and build that muscle so that bigger responsibilities don't feel as heavy.

In my book, *She's Just Another Navy Pilot* (USNI Publishing, 2000), I describe the difficulties of being one of the first women to deploy in a combat squadron in the Navy onboard an aircraft carrier. Being a naval aviator is challenging enough. While it's incredibly fulfilling and fun, the job of flying jets is demanding, unforgiving, and probably the toughest challenge and biggest responsibility I've taken on in my life, other than being a parent. Add to that the acute pressure of feeling like I was representing

ALL women as I performed my duties, and you can imagine how intense those years were.

Fortunately, I was raised by two Marines. Responsibility was a quality that, if not innate, was certainly imbued in me by my parents.

When I was 12 years old, I tried out for the Little League baseball team. There were two divisions, major league and minor league. I had two brothers who were baseball fanatics, so I had practiced many hours with them and thought I'd be good enough to make the major league. Unfortunately, I was placed on a minor league team — with a bunch of eight-year-old boys whom I towered over. For an adolescent girl, this was about as embarrassing as it gets.

I wanted to quit the team. I even "forgot" to tell my mom and dad when my team practice was. This did not go over well with my parents. They emphasized the importance of honoring commitments and sticking with a team, even when it wasn't going how I wanted it to.

Twelve-year-old me. The only time I smiled while wearing this baseball uniform.
Photo Credit. Author

I stayed with the team for the entire season. I'd like to say that I learned to love the little twerps I played with but honestly, I was thrilled when the last strike was called in our final game, and I no longer had to play on that team.

Even though I was glad to be done, in the back of my pre-teen mind I recognized that I had strengthened a mental muscle, the same muscle that would help me many years later when I was trying to land for the fourth time on a dark and stormy night on the aircraft carrier. That muscle was the ability to be responsible.

Responsibility to Self

One of the common themes I see with my coaching clients is the desire to be better communicators. It includes "front-of-the-room" or "executive" presence — many business leaders need support with that type of development — but I mean the ability to clearly articulate needs.

In Chapter 2 we looked at self-awareness and how to better understand what matters most to you. Once you know your values, it's your responsibility to live a life that honors them. It might feel easier to wait for others to provide for those needs, but then if they don't, it's also much easier to lay the blame on them than take personal responsibility. Responsibility to self means having the courage and the self-respect to stand up for yourself and what's important in your life.

Responsibility to Others

When something feels "off" in a conversation, we notice it. Human beings are social creatures, and we have the ability to be tuned in to each other. However, we often don't name it because we are afraid of conflict, and we'd rather avoid it and hope it goes away. As my coach, Rick Tamlyn, says in his usual catchy way, "You need to name the trauma to release the drama."

When you are SOARing, you will notice these incongruencies like bumps of turbulence — the unsteady movement of air in violent motion. Checking in with the other person is the opportunity to fly out together to a smoother altitude.

We've been told that using the collective pronoun "we" helps us to be more inclusive and "team-focused," but I encourage you to think about how you use it. I think it's good to use "we" when referring to team success and accomplishments, but "I" when talking about things that haven't gone well. Saying "I" instead shows responsibility, rather than hiding your accountability behind others.

What's in *your* control equals what *you're* responsible for:

- Your thoughts and actions
- Your inner dialogue
- How you handle challenges
- How you handle negative emotions
- Your boundaries
- Where and how you spend your energy
- Your goals

What's out of your control:

- The past
- The future
- What other people do
- What other people think
- How other people feel about you

Overview Effect

Astronauts and cosmonauts experience this when they've been in space, looking back at our planet. It's a change in perspective, a feeling of awe, and a sense of responsibility when they are looking at our planet from space.

One can experience this effect when flying at 35,000 feet or higher with a 60-degree field of view — something we see in jet cockpits but not as a passenger on an airliner. When I flew F/A-18 Hornets, I had the opportunity to fly at a high enough altitude to see a tiny bit of the curvature of the earth. I don't think my experience was as profound as the astronauts', but I definitely felt something.

When I looked down and realized that everything I've ever experienced in life has happened on the planet below me, I felt both small and insignificant as well as very connected to the other human beings in our world.

As a speaker and trainer, I help clients perform their own "overview," pulling them out of the minutiae of their everyday activities and supporting them to create time where they can reflect on their life and what they want to get out of it. It's easy to blame our jobs, bosses, parents, partners, kids — whomever you want to choose — for stifling our dreams or not supporting our desires for what we want in life, but the truth is that it's our own responsibility to make it happen, not theirs.

I was a theater nerd in high school. I loved being on a stage, behind the stage, writing plays… I geeked out on all of it. During my freshman year of college at the University of San Diego, I participated in a school-sponsored trip to Los Angeles to see the musical *Cats*. I could not believe what I was seeing… I'd never seen a professional musical before and This. Was. INSANE. to me. The singing was incredible, the dancing was mind-blowing, the costumes, the lighting, all of it… took my breath away. Yes, I laughed, I cried… it was, uh, well, it was *Cats*! I was enthralled by all of it, and I remember riding the bus home to San Diego thinking, *How can I be a part of that world?*

Unfortunately, there was a huge obstacle at the time that kept me from dropping out of college and pursuing an acting career — Tom and Sandi Draude, my parents. They viewed my love for theater as a "hobby" and believed I was better suited for a career in the military as a leader. They indulged my love for musicals, even taking me to see *A Chorus Line* for my 18th birthday. Seeing that particular musical, about actors hoping to be cast in a show, right about the same time as I saw *Cats*, felt like a sign from God (I was still a practicing Catholic at that point in my life). But I knew my parents probably wouldn't be supportive. Still, I had to try to convince them.

I called them from my resident assistant's dorm room because she had one of the long phone cords that extended out of her room and into the stairwell, where I could have some privacy. I was afraid to tell my parents that I had changed my mind about being in the Naval Reserve Officer Training Corps (NROTC) and that I wanted to change my major to theater and go into acting. My parents meant the world to me and knowing this would disappoint them was eating me up. But I told them. And they told me there was no way in hell they'd support it, financially or morally. There was a cognitive dissonance in how they both looked down on acting as a profession but loved certain actors, like Jimmy Stewart and Bette Davis.

I wasn't strong enough yet to go against my parents' wishes, so I stayed in NROTC, but I participated in plays in college. I took advantage of my fairly consistent flight school schedule and performed in community theater before I got to the fleet, where my schedule was too unpredictable to commit to participating in a show.

For many years, I held a grudge against my parents for "squashing my dream." But the truth is I let them squash it. If

I'd had courage and faith in myself, I would have accepted their disapproval and done it anyway. I didn't take responsibility for that decision for many years.

It's funny how the things we truly desire often find a way into our lives. I couldn't do community theater while I was based on an aircraft carrier, but while we were out at sea, I was an enthusiastic participant in our "Foc's'le Follies," where our air wing squadrons gathered together to perform funny skits or musical parody numbers, poking fun at each other and the navy. I even started writing a musical parody of West Side Story called "Top Side Story" about life on the flight deck of an aircraft carrier. Obviously, there was a song called "Jets": "When you fly jets, you fly jets all the way, from your first carrier qual to your last flying day…" I also wrote a song to the tune of Maria – "A Helo": "A helo… I just flew a bird called a helo, and suddenly the ground, will never feel so sound to me. A helo, say it loud and there's rotors flailing, say it's soft and it's almost like praying, oh Jesus, don't let the nut fly off my helo…"

When I left the service, I applied to both business schools and film schools. The music videos I'd made for my squadron helped me get accepted to one of the best film schools in the country, USC, but I talked myself out of it. Once again, I let fear keep me from honoring my creative side. I didn't think I'd be successful moving to a completely new industry that on the surface felt very different from the military. Business school seemed like the safer choice.

At business school, I zeroed in on The Wharton Follies, the school's annual musical I described in Chapter 3. Participating in the cast and writing team was one of my favorite parts about going to school at Wharton.

When I entered the corporate world after business school, I again put my creative dreams on hold, although now that I think about it, I did sing with company bands when I worked at Bain & Company and at Military.com.

Once my youngest child was in high school, I got back on a stage. I wrote a one-woman show about my experience as one of the first women to fly combat jets in the navy. I debuted the show Off-Broadway in 2021, performed it at the Edinburgh Fringe Festival in 2022, and again at the Hollywood Fringe Festival in 2023. I felt like I'd finally achieved my dream of becoming an actor, and what enabled me to do so was my experience flying jets. Crazy, right? Strangely enough, the more I've learned about acting and the film industry, the more I see the similarities between putting on a show or filming a feature, and the effort and coordination to launch aircraft off a ship.

"Performing 'I Feel the Need' off-Broadway at the United Solo Festival in November 2021." Photo credit: Scotty Perkins

I took a very long path to being responsible for doing something that really matters to me. While I loved serving in the navy and flying off an aircraft carrier, there was always a longing to participate in something creative. It was much easier, when I was younger, to blame my parents instead of admitting that my fear was holding me back. Now that I'm a parent, I understand that they were being protective of me and directing me towards a career where they felt I'd be successful. I don't blame them at all. They're now 100 percent behind my creative pursuits and I'm grateful for their support.

Your Flight Plan

1. Write your obituary. Date it on the day of your 108th birthday and start documenting the legacy you want to leave behind. How do you make this planet and the people on it better?

2. Write a letter to your future self. I love the website futureme. org because you can send yourself an email that will get delivered months or years in the future. Write about what you hope the future you is doing and being. Check in with how you're feeling in the present.

3. This exercise is built upon an example from Jack Canfield's website about taking 100 percent responsibility for your life.[12] In the arena of your life, think about an area where you want to be better and where you want to be more responsible.

Areas of your life include:

- Family and Friends
- Significant Other/Romance

12 https://jackcanfield.com/blog/taking-100-responsibility-for-your-life/

- Work/Career, Financial
- Health, Fun/Recreation
- Physical Environment and Personal Growth

Reflecting on this area, ask yourself the following questions:

- What is a difficult or troubling situation in your life?
- How are you creating it or allowing it to happen?
- What are you pretending not to know?
- What is the payoff for keeping it like it is?
- What would you rather be experiencing?
- What actions will you take to create that?
- By when will you take that action?

> *"Being responsible means accepting that you are the cause and the solution of the matter."*
>
> —JACK CANFIELD

Chapter 6

CONCLUSION

I've used the acronym SOAR as a convenient way to summarize the concepts that I've found helpful in my own life. "Soaring" is living with joy and purpose.

The technicality of soaring is meaningful to me as well as the acronym.

Glider pilots use thermals to soar. Thermals are columns of rising air from the ground that are formed through the warming of the surface by sunlight. You've seen the results of thermals when there's enough moisture in the air… the water from the thermal condenses and forms cumulus clouds. If you've ever seen a bird staying aloft without flapping its wings, it's using a thermal to soar.

I think of this as an analogy for ways that people can take advantage of uplifting powerful energy in their life, similar to a thermal. Basically, if you can stay in a thermal, it will provide continuous upward lift and keep you flying. If you don't have that force beneath you, the soaring stops and you'll start falling from the sky. Then you'll have to start flapping those wings and working harder to stay aloft!

When I say the word soar you might also hear, "sore," which I think is also relevant because it reminds me of how my muscles feel the day after working them hard. Change is tough, and if we're not pushing ourselves a little sometimes, we're not going to get stronger, physically or mentally. Also, you wouldn't expect to go into a gym if you haven't been working out and immediately be able to bench press twice your body weight the first day. We need to build up strength over time. I hope you do find yourself a little "sore" as you stretch yourself and start living the life you want.

There are three ways to live life: believing that life happens to you, that life happens for you, or that life happens through you. When you think that life happens *to* you, you are taking a victim's perspective and giving up on your own responsibility to influence your life. When you believe that life can happen *for* you, you view your life as a learning journey where you're experiencing personal growth and even though you might not know why or how you believe there's a divine influence. Finally, when you can think of life as happening *through* you, you're expanding that growth to the world and recognizing the divine within you. When we SOAR, life is happening through us.

Why I Soar

Anyone who's seen the movie *Saving Private Ryan* will remember the final scene. I don't know a single veteran who can make it through that scene without tearing up with emotion. Private Ryan, as an older man, asks his wife if he's a good man and if he's lived a good life. He wants to make sure his buddies' sacrifices to get him home weren't wasted.

I often think about the people from my air wing who died while we served together:

Lt. Kara "Hulk" Hultgreen
Lt. Glenn "K-9" Kersgieter
Lt. Cdr. Stacy "Sprout" Bates

Lt. Graham "Hobbs" Higgins
Lt. Cdr. Bill "B. B." Breaker
Lt. Cdr. James "Jimmy D" Dee
Lt. Tom Francis
Lt. Larry "Jedi" Anderson

I'm honoring their sacrifices by living my best life and enjoying the freedom and privilege I experience from being an American.

I hope this book has inspired you to live your best life: a life you love and are grateful for, and in turn, inspire the people in your life, whether it's people you work with, your friends and family or your community.

I encourage you to share your own stories with the people you care about. We learn from each other through our stories, and if we don't share them, our stories will die with us.

Tomorrow is not guaranteed. The time to live a life you love is now. Find your thermals and SOAR.

Resources aka The "Gouge"

The gouge is the inside scoop, the unofficial guidance, the knowledge that is passed from experienced aviators to the FNGs (new guys/gals). I was introduced to the naval aviation term "the gouge" while in NROTC (Naval Reserve Officer Training Corps) in college.

There's a saying "Live by the gouge, die by the gouge," which means you better trust the person who is giving you gouge because if their gouge is out of date or unreliable, you're out of luck.

Gouge is especially important in naval aviation because our manuals specify what we're *not* allowed to do. The implication is that if the manual doesn't say not to do it, you can do it. Contrast that with the Air Force, whose manuals state what they're allowed to do, and, therefore, if it's not in the manual, you cannot do it. We naval aviators like to think this means we're more entrepreneurial and creative than our Air Force counterparts, since there's so much possibility outside of what's restricted versus being able to only do what's allowed.

For naval aviators, the gouge provides tips and tricks that enable us to navigate our way through that wide-open world of what's not prohibited.

I appreciate that if you've made it to this chapter that you've read a lot and it might be helpful to have an easy-to-use summary of what I've shared. This is where the gouge comes in.

Below are bulleted points that distill down the lessons I've learned and shared and recommendations for books I've found intriguing and illuminating. I hope you'll find it a helpful reference tool that will enable you to keep soaring when you're feeling the weight of the world drag you down.

Rowdy's Gouge:

- FAIL = **F**irst **A**ttempt **i**n **L**earning
- FEAR = **F**uture **E**vents **A**ren't **R**eal
- Know who you are and what matters most to you.
- Be true to yourself. Don't pretend to be someone you're not.
- Comparing yourself to anyone else is a waste of your time. There's only one unique, amazing you.
- It's normal to feel fear. It's a biological protection mechanism.
- Don't spend too much time and energy worrying about making the right decision; instead, make a decision and then make it right.
- Being vulnerable requires strength; it is not weakness.
- Name the trauma to release the drama. Be honest with yourself about what's going on inside when you feel negative emotions.
- It's great to feel appreciation, it's even better to share it with someone you appreciate.
- Your candle does not burn brighter by blowing out someone else's.
- We choose how we show up in the world and how we respond to negative emotions.

Rowdy's Book Recommendations

S: Self-Awareness: Remind yourself that you're awesome and can accomplish things that are difficult:

You Are a Badass by Jen Sincero
The Big Leap by Gay Hendricks
Everything is Figureoutable by Marie Forleo
Untamed by Glennon Doyle
Man's Search for Meaning by Victor Frankl
Playing Big by Tara Mohr

O: Openness: Challenge your perspectives and explore new ways of viewing the world:

Just Work by Kim Scott
The Surrender Experiment by Michael Singer
The Power of Now by Eckhardt Tolle
Caste by Isabel Williamson
Me and White Supremacy by Layla Saad
So You Want to Talk About Race by Ijeoma Oluo
White Fragility by Robin DiAngelo

A: Appreciation: Recognizing and cultivating the good things in our lives

The Artist's Way by Julia Cameron
Radical Compassion by Tara Brach
The Soul of Money by Lynne Twist

R: Responsibility: Own and improve your behavior and emotions

Atomic Habits by James Clear
Getting Things Done by David Allen
Positive Intelligence by Shirzad Chamine
Four Thousand Weeks: Time Management for Mortals by Oliver
    Burkeman

Miscellaneous

Leadership:

The Four F's of Leadership by BGEN T.V. Draude, USMC (Ret.)
Co-Active Leadership by Karen and Henry Kimsey-House
Leadership and Self-Deception by The Arbinger Institute

Communication:

Co-Active Coaching by Henry Kimsey-House, Karen Kimsey
    House, Phillip Sandhal, and Laura Whitworth
Nonviolent Communication by Marshall Rosenberg
Crucial Conversations by Kerry Patterson, Joseph Grenny,
    Ron McMillan, and Al Switzler
Atlas of the Heart by Brené Brown
Radical Candor by Kim Scott

Acknowledgments

This is where I get to exercise the "A" in SOAR. I am grateful to the many, many people in my life who have supported me in my soaring journey. Anyone who has offered encouraging words or sent positive vibes my way has contributed to lifting me up in this world. Thank you.

I am grateful to Tom and Sandi Draude, Patrick Draude, Ryan Draude, Scotty Perkins, Harry Hirschman and Cari Costanzo, who read drafts of this book and offered their sage feedback.

I'm also thankful for my incredible coach, Rick Tamlyn, and his crackerjack team — his husband, Chuck Lioi, and their Wonder Woman business associate, Jocelynn Flowers, as well as the entire ProduceU community. I'm grateful for Rick's guidance, creativity, and light.

I've experienced many phases of my life (growing up, college, the Navy, business school, tech career, single parenthood, coach, artist, empty nester) in different places (Pensacola, Kingsville, Lemoore, San Diego, Philadelphia, Palo Alto, New York City) and I've been fortunate to meet many wonderful people along the way. I'm even luckier that I've built relationships with so many smart, kind, and funny people who became and remain my close friends. You know who you are and I'm grateful for you.

The development of this book is bookended by two great teams. On the front end, Dan Janal helped me kick it off in the winter of 2019/2020. Looking at the Pacific Ocean is a great way to write, and Dan and his wife were kind enough to invite me to work on the book from their condo in San Diego. We all know what happened in the world between 2020 and 2022; for me, this book took a backseat to other priorities during that time. Earlier in 2023, Rick encouraged me to pick up my book again and connected me with the team at Hybrid Global Publishing. Karen Strauss has wisely guided me through this process along with Karina Cooke. Claudia Volkman patiently waited for me to get through a run of my one-woman show so I could focus on finishing the book and I am thankful for her editing prowess. Julia Kuris designed the gorgeous cover and my friend Chris Wojcicki designed my logo.

My parents have done a 180 from when I was in high school, and I told them I want to be an actor. We've all grown and become more accepting of the fact that we can't control others' choices. I am fortunate to have a supportive family, including my brothers, Patrick and Ryan, my sisters-in-law, Kristin and Despina, my nieces, Priya and Leena, and, of course, the lights of my life, my son, Sam, and daughter, Julia. My family are my biggest cheerleaders as I indulge my creative curiosities, and I am grateful for their love and support.

Finally, I appreciate you, dear reader! Thank you for picking up my book. I hope you are inspired to SOAR in your life. I would love to hear from you: loree@loreedraude.com

About the Author

Loree earned her commission through the NROTC program at the University of San Diego, where she majored in mathematics. She began her naval aviation career as a support pilot at VAQ-34, flying F/A-18 Hornets at Naval Air Station Lemoore in California. When the Combat Exclusion Policy for women was repealed, Loree transitioned to a combat jet aviation squadron where she flew the S-3B Viking and completed two six-month deployments to the Persian Gulf on the *USS Abraham Lincoln* and the *USS Kitty Hawk*. Besides piloting jet aircraft, Loree was a division officer responsible for leading teams of enlisted sailors, and was the squadron's aviation safety officer, responsible for ensuring her squadron followed safe operating procedures. During her second deployment, she became the first woman air wing-qualified landing signal officer (LSO), a role awarded to a small percentage of naval aviators for the responsibility of helping fixed-wing pilots land safely on the carrier.

Loree spent over a year of her life deployed at sea and accumulated over 300 carrier landings, including 99 at night.

She completed her naval aviation career as a fleet replacement squadron instructor pilot, where she taught newly winged naval aviators how to fly the S-3B Viking and land it on an aircraft carrier. She also led the largest division in the squadron — a team of over 100 aircraft maintenance technicians.

After her naval service, Loree earned an MBA at the Wharton School of The University of Pennsylvania. She spent 20 years in Silicon Valley, leading teams at startups and tech companies, including Google and Meta, in marketing, operations, and customer support organizations. In 2020, she started her own executive coaching and leadership development business to support leaders and teams in the tech industry. She is the host of the Supersonic Leaders and Teams podcast and a certified yoga instructor.

Loree wrote a one-woman show called *I Feel the Need* about the first West Coast aircraft carrier deployment with women in combat squadrons. Directed by Beth Bornstein Dunnington, the show debuted Off-Broadway at the 2021 United Solo Theatre Festival in NYC, where it sold out and won the award for Best Direction. Loree performed her show 23 times at the 2022 Edinburgh Fringe Festival and, in 2023, performed it at the Hollywood Fringe Festival where it was nominated for several awards.

Loree has been laid off, forced to shut down her startup due to lack of funding, been divorced, fired, and quit her job. She also overuses commas in her writing.

When she is not supporting leaders or speaking onstage, she enjoys painting (www.encaustech.com), traveling, yoga, hiking, and flying.

Services

Activational speaker: Loree inspires audiences of all sizes and supports leaders and teams to reach peak performance. Her interactive keynotes are highly engaging and inspire audiences to soar higher professionally and personally. If you are looking for an entertaining and motivational speaker, contact Loree.

Executive coaching and leadership development: Loree has coached hundreds of executives, leaders and entrepreneurs in Silicon Valley tech companies, startups and the military. She has also supported teams to work together more effectively and improve their communication and teamwork skills. Loree customizes her coaching and training programs to suit your desired outcomes.

One-woman show: In her award-winning play, *I Feel the Need,* Loree takes to the cockpit again and brings the audience along on a G-force trip as she lands on an aircraft carrier and recounts the adventure, humor and tragedy she experienced during the historic deployment on the U.S.S. Abraham Lincoln.

For more information, visit www.loreedraude.com

Follow Loree on Social Media:

Instagram: www.instagram.com/loreedraude

Facebook: www.facebook.com/loreedraude

Scan the QR code below for updates on Loree's offers and events:

www.ingramcontent.com/pod-product-compliance
Lightning Source LLC
Chambersburg PA
CBHW030924140626
46545CB00016B/2349